The Big
Book of
BUDS

The Big Book of **BUDS**

volume **4**

Marijuana Varieties from the World's Great Seed Breeders

Edited by Ed Rosenthal

Quick American Publishing

Big Book of Buds Volume 4
Copyright 2010 Quick Trading Company

Photographs of varieties in The Big Book of Buds 4 appear courtesy of the contributors. All other photos by Ed Rosenthal, unless otherwise credited.

Published by Quick American Publishing
A division of Quick Trading Company
9 Lake Ave., Piedmont, California
ISBN 13: 978-0-932551-48-1

Executive Editor: Ed Rosenthal
Project Editor: S. Newhart
Project Manager: Jack Jennings
Design: Scott Idleman/Blink
Art & Photo Direction: Hera Lee
Editorial Assistance: Angela Bacca
Copyeditor: Cindy Jennings
Proofreader: Leslie Kwartin
Cover Photo: Crippled Pit, courtesy of Stoney Girl Gardens

Printed in China

Variety descriptions and breeder stories compiled by S. Newhart with the assistance of Angela Bacca.

We wish to thank all the Big Book of Buds 4 contributors for providing articles, information and photos. Without your participation and support, this book would not have been possible.

Publisher's Cataloging-in-Publication
(Provided by Quality Books, Inc.)

The big book of buds. Volume 4, Marijuana varieties from
    the world's great seed breeders / edited by Ed Rosenthal.
        p. cm.
        Includes bibliographical references and index.
        ISBN-13: 978-0932551481
        ISBN-10: 0932551483

    1. Cannabis. 2. Marijuana.   I. Rosenthal, Ed.

SB295.C35B54 2010   633.7'9
QBI10-600151

Try your bookstore first but you may order this book from our website—*www.quicktrading.com*

This volume is dedicated to Marc Emery, who is presently in prison for defending freedom in North America.

She can dance a Cajun rhythm,
Jump like a Willys in 4-wheel drive,
She's a summer love for spring, fall and winter,
She can make happy anyone alive...
She's got everything delightful,
She's got everything I need,
A breeze in the pines and the sun and bright moonlight,
Lazing in the sunlight, yes indeed.

From "Sugar Magnolia"
Words by Robert Hunter, Bob Weir
Reproduced by arrangement with Ice Nine Publishing Co., Inc.
(ASCAP)

Contents

Introduction

By Ed Rosenthal

Marijuana is an amazing plant. It's the proverbial outlaw that is now gaining respectability. Marijuana bends the rules, breaks the rules, and ignores the rules in so many ways: some are obvious and some are obscure. Marijuana defies authority. It has been outlawed, condemned, and "eradicated" many times. Despite these hardships it comes back to change society.

Most recreational drugs blunt your thinking. Alcohol, most pills and opiates take you away from reality to a duller, more comfortable place. Marijuana forces the world on you in surreal colors. It stops your mind from filtering thoughts, so more bubbles up into consciousness. Instead of inhibiting thought, marijuana expands perception, encouraging ingenuity. It may also unmask the absurdity of laws that criminalize an unadulterated, free growing plant. In many cases, humans who become allied with marijuana also become its unrepentant defenders, defying authority when authority is clearly working against a more enlightened and truthful approach to cannabis.

Most domesticated plants, such as corn and wheat, are dependent on humans. They have lost their ability to live on their own—to go feral. Not so for cannabis. It has gone feral more than once, and while it has a symbiotic relationship with humans it is always ready to take off on its own should its companions abandon it.

Marijuana has also conquered territory few other plants could before: "The Great Indoors." As the world becomes more urbanized, farming is becoming more isolated and fewer people are engaged in it. Marijuana has created a new generation of urban farmers. With the exception of an occasional tomato or pepper plant, few other plants have proliferated indoors the way marijuana has.

Only a few large agricultural companies are involved in breeding most plants. Because most types of fruits, vegetables, and flowers are commercialized, we are accustomed to seeing only a few varieties, and few hobby gardeners attempt to cross breed. By contrast, marijuana is a plant that encourages amateur breeding. Marijuana is the only annual plant that is dioecious. It has separate male and female plants. No other annual plant has this characteristic. At a basic botanical level, this makes marijuana breeding more paint-by-numbers than almost any other hobby plant.

As an outlaw plant for most of the last century, marijuana has passed hand to hand, and its cultivation has spawned thousands of breeders. Most of them are not commercial. They are just making a cross or two to see what happens. The commercial breeders, those whose achievements are depicted in this book, are also an anomaly. Instead of becoming more concentrated, the seed industry has expanded as more and more breeders have gone commercial and are bringing the fruits of their labor to market. This is exactly the opposite of what is happening in the world of commercial seed breeding of other plants, where the number of companies involved in commercial breeding continues to shrink.

The resulting quality of the plants has also improved. They have been adapted to specific environments and are easier to cultivate, produce higher yields, and mature more quickly than their predecessors.

So here we are. This book, the fourth edition in the series, heralds a new maturity in seed breeding. The early crosses are called "old school." The effects are getting more sophisticated, exploring new areas and turning us on in new ways.

This book represents the newest chapter in a rapidly evolving industry. But that does not do the phenomenon justice. It is much more than an industry. This book records the result of the passion, labor, and insight that continues to create new varieties with more flavors and nuances to offer the aficionado. All are guaranteed to turn your head.

The icon sections can be used as a quick key to varieties. Buds 3 added the feminized seed, and new to Buds 4 is an icon that indicates whether a variety is autoflowering. Each icon is described here in detail.

The Icons

The first icon deals with plant type. The possibilities are:

S   represents plants with over 90% sativa background

I   represents plants with over 90% indica background

Hybrids which are:

S I   more sativa

I S   more indica

S   Sativa plants grow from the equator through the 50th parallel. They include both marijuana and hemp varieties. The plants that interest marijuana growers come from the equator to the 20th parallel. Countries from this area are noted for high-grade marijuana and include Colombia, Jamaica, Nigeria, Congo, Thailand and Sumatra. Populations of plants from most of these areas are quite uniform for several reasons. Cannabis is not native to these areas. It was imported to grow hemp crops and then it adapted over many generations with human intervention. Each population originated from a small amount of fairly uniform seed from the 45–50th parallel. Then the populations evolved over hundreds of generations with the help of humans. This led to fairly uniform populations in climates that varied little year to year.

Sativas grow into 5–15 feet (1.5–4.5 meters) tall symmetrical pine-shaped plants. The spaces between the leaves on the stem, the internodes, are longer on sativas than indicas. This helps to give sativas a taller stature. The lowest branches are the widest, spreading 1½ to 3 feet (.5–1 meter); since the branches grow opposite each other, plant diameter may reach 6 feet (1.8 meters). The leaves are long, slender, and fingerlike. The plants are light green since they contain less chlorophyll.

Sativa buds are lighter than indicas. Some varieties grow buds along the entire branch, developing a thin but dense cola. Others grow large formations of more loose, spongy buds. The smoke is sweet and spicy or fruity. The highs are described as soaring, psychedelic, thoughtful, and spacy.

I   Indica plants originated around the 30th parallel in the Hindu Kush region of the Himalayan foothills. This includes the countries of Afghanistan, Pakistan, Tajikistan, Northern India, and Nepal. The weather there is quite variable from year to year. For this reason the populations in these regions have a varied gene pool. Even within a particular population there is a high degree of heterogeneity, which results in plants of the same variety having quite a bit of variability. This helps the population survive. No matter what the weather during a particular year, some plants will thrive and reproduce.

These plants are fairly short, usually under 5 feet (1.5 meters) tall. They are bushy with compact branching and short internodes. They range in shape from a rounded bush to a pine-like shape with a wide base. The leaves are short, very wide, and dark green when compared to most equatorial sativas because they contain larger amounts of chlorophyll. Sometimes there is webbing between the leaflets. At the 30th latitude, the plants don't receive as much light as plants at or near the equator. By increasing the amount of chlorophyll, the cells use light more efficiently.

Indica buds are dense and tight. They form several shapes depending on variety. All of them are chunky or blocky. Sometimes they form continuous clusters along the stem. They have intense smells ranging from acrid, skunky, or musky to deep pungent aromas reminiscent of chocolate, coffee, earth, or hash. Indica smoke is dense, lung expanding, and cough inducing. The high is heavy, body-oriented, and lethargic.

 a sativa-dominant variety crossed with auto-flowering ruderalis

 an indica-dominant variety crossed with autoflowering ruderalis

 a combination of sativa, indica, and ruderalis genetics

R Ruderalis hybrids: In recent years, it has become more common to hear of the ruderalis variant of cannabis alongside indica and sativa. First encountered in Russia, ruderalis was named in 1924 and was often referred to as "weedy" cannabis because it was low in THC content and high in cannabidiol (CBD). Ruderalis plants are found in the wild in the far northern portions of the Caucuses Mountains and areas north of the 40th parallel in western Asia. Even though its smoke is nothing to brag about, ruderalis has one unique quality that has saved it from the trash bin of history. Unlike other forms of cannabis that require changes to the light cycle in order to begin flowering, ruderalis flowers automatically. More and more breeding projects are working with this cannabis subspecies to create autoflowering varieties.

IS Indica-sativa hybrids naturally tend towards the indica side of the family. They usually have controlled height. They don't grow very tall and after forcing flowering, their growth is limited. Their side branching is usually not prominent and they can be grown in a small space. However, since they have both sativa and indica influences, they may include surprising hints of sativa in some aspect of the plant's makeup, the flavors, or the high.

SI Sativa-indica hybrids tend towards the sativa parentage. They are taller plants, which will grow to double or triple their size if they are forced when they are small. They are usually hard to grow in a sea of green, as the plants demand more space to spread out. However, the indica genetics may influence the size of the plant or its buds, the speed of flowering, the density of buds, the flavors, or the high.

The pure ruderalis is a short plant. It does not typically exceed a height of 1.5 feet (50 cm). It often grows as a single-stem plant, forming wide leaves and pinecone sized colas. Because of its size, ruderalis is sometimes called "bonsai" cannabis. Its smaller size also means it matures much more rapidly than most indicas and sativas. This was probably an adaptation to the short grow season of the Russian steppes. While pure ruderalis varieties do not possess enough desirable qualities to be commercially viable, ruderalis crosses abound right now in the marketplace. Most plants will have a more rapid season and form a shorter plant when crossed with ruderalis. In addition, ruderalis becomes synonymous with autoflowering varieties.

Because of their short growing season, these varieties have adapted by beginning to flower soon after germination. Flowering peaks by mid-summer and seeds drop before the first frost. The plants will begin to flower without being regulated by the light cycle. This characteristic seems to be dominant and is easily transferred to hybrids. Very often hybrids will have a small percentage of plants that are not autoflowering. Although flowering is not initiated by shorter days, flower growth is stimulated if there is some light deprivation, as few as 8 or 10 hours a day of uninterrupted darkness can increase flower growth considerably. Usually these plants go from germination to completion of flowering within 100–110 days.

With the many combinations and complex parentages of modern hybrids, it is impossible to generalize about the qualities of hybrids' smoke, highs, or other characteristics. So many plants have been crossed and their progeny used for breeding that it is truly a mixed-up world out there. The *Big Book of Buds* series answers your questions regarding characteristics of particular varieties.

The Buzz icon is the one that is most important to me. What is the high like? Describing a state of mind is not an easy task. Separating one's mental state from the state of mind created by the brain's interplay with cannabinoids is subtle. We have used many terms to describe this state:

active • alert • balanced • blissful • body relaxation • body stone • calm • cerebral • cheerful •clear (headed) • couchlock • creative • creeper • dreamy • energetic • euphoric • even head/body high • fast • functional • giggly • happy • hazy • heady • inspirational • intense • introspective • lively • lethargic • lucid • mellow • munchies • narcotic • pain relief • physically relaxing • playful • positive • psychedelic • sedative • sensual • sleepy • soaring • social • stoney • talkative • thoughtful • trippy • uplifting • visual • wandering mind

These descriptions attempt to capture the elusive qualities of the high and are based on a typical response; however, each person has a unique relationship with marijuana, which means his or her response to a strain may range outside of the typical. The text contains more complete descriptions.

The Taste/Smell icon is a short one to three word description of the smell and taste. Some of the odors included are:

acrid • berry • bubblegum • candy • chocolate • citrus • coffee • creamy • earthy • floral • fruit • hashy • herbal • honey • incense • mango • melon • musky • nutty • peppery • pine • pineapple • piney • pungent • sandalwood • skunk • smooth • spicy • sweet • tobacco • tropical sweet • vanilla • woodsy

The Flowering Time icon details the number of days it takes the plant to ripen after forcing flowering. Some outdoor strains also offer the approximate time of harvest. Both environmental conditions and subjective factors affect maturation.

Take, for instance, one experiment in which identical plants grown indoors in a lab were fed different water-soluble commercial fertilizers. These identical plants grown under identical conditions except the fertilizers ripened up to 10 days apart. The fertilizers also affected the taste and quality of the buds.

Plant growth and maturation is also affected by temperature. Both cold and hot conditions interfere with ripening. Temperate conditions encourage fast growth and prompt ripening. The planting method is another factor that affects ripening time. Hydroponic plants mature earlier than their sisters in planting medium.

I would call a plant ripe when the "resin" in the glands starts to turn milky or amber. This is about a week later than some people prefer. The taste differs and the cannabinoids may change a bit, resulting in different highs. Dutch coffee shops often sell bud that is immature. The glands are there, but have not filled completely with THC. The high is racing and buzzy. I don't find it that satisfying. Obviously, ripening time is affected by your idea of ripeness.

It is easy to see that the numbers mentioned are intended to give the reader an approximation rather than hard figures. While they offer an indication of what you should expect, they shouldn't be used to figure your timetable.

The Yield icon is a report of expected yield. These figures are somewhat ambiguous since the results are not reported consistently. Cannabis, like all green plants, uses light to fuel photosynthesis. The sugars produced become tissue. As a shortcut, you could say Light = Growth. Yields vary first and foremost due to light conditions, so space or plant definitions are incomplete by themselves. The yields that appear here assume that indoor gardens are receiving at least 600 watts per meter (wpm) where no light wattage is indicated.

The Parents icon is the parentage of the variety. While this can get quite complex, you get an idea of what the possibilities are for any variety by knowing its parents.

Some of the hybrids in the book are F2 unstabilized. When pure strains (let's call them strains A & B) are crossed and a hybrid is produced, the first generation, the F1 hybrid plants, are all uniform because they all contain the same genes. One set from the female and one set from the male. When two F1's are crossed, the seeds receive a random assortment of genes. For each of the more than 100,000 sets of genes, a plant may get two genes from A, one each from A and B, or two from B. No two plants are alike.

To stabilize them so that they have similar characteristics, the plants are inbred for five or six generations creating an F6, using careful selections. However breeders often work with unstabilized hybrids, which has an advantage when breeding for cloning.

Stability can be judged in part by the number of parents a variety has. Pure strains are the most uniform, since they are not recombining different genetic dispositions. Hybrids have the advantage of gaining vigor from the fresh combination. They also vary more. Strains with three or four parents are likely to exhibit more than one phenotype when grown out. When the three parents are hybrids themselves, the combination can result in quite a bit of diversity.

Diversity is not bad. Consider a gardener starting out. Clones are taken once the plants grow some side stems. When the plants have been harvested and tasted the gardener decides to select two plants for the next garden. Clones of those plants are grown vegetatively and used for mothers. If the seed line were uniform as it is with pure strains or stabilized varieties, there would not be much difference between the plants. Seeds from an unstabilized variety give the gardener more choices.

The following icons indicate recommendations for planting. The choices are:

 indoor

 outdoor

 indoor/outdoor

Outdoor strains may do well in a greenhouse setup, but will be difficult to grow indoors. They may require too much light for inside growing, and usually have their own ideas about growth and height, making them hard to tame. The problem with most plants not recommended for outdoors in temperate climates is the plants don't ripen by the end of the season. Some plants rated as indoor plants can be grown outdoors if they are forced to flower early using shade cloth. As an example, a plant which ripens in mid-November, 45 days after a gardener's September 30th harvest schedule, could be coaxed to flower early by covering it with opaque plastic each evening after sunset. Remove the cover 12 hours after sunset, beginning in late spring or early summer. Most varieties will ripen within 60–70 days.

Plants that are recommended for growing outdoors indicate the maturity date under natural light. When no latitude is mentioned, figure the month indicated is at the same latitude as the country of origin. For Holland, the latitude is 52° N. Canadian seeds are produced at the 50° N latitude, U.S. seeds at the 38° N latitude, and Spanish seeds are produced at the 40–41° N latitude. More can be learned about outdoor harvest times and latitude in the appendixes. Also read Franco's article on drying and curing (page 170) to discover how these processes influence the flavor and the high.

This icon only appears on varieties that have been feminized. Feminized seeds are the result of a cross between a regular female and male induced pollen on a second female, resulting in 100% female seeds. Feminized seeds are great for the gardener that does not want to sex plants. Breeders may want a mix of male and female seeds for their purposes. Some varieties are only available in a feminized form, while other breeders offer both regular and feminized versions of the same strains to suit the needs of different gardening projects.

This icon only appears on varieties that are autoflowering. While most varieties of domesticated marijuana fall into the major categories of indica or sativa, the autoflowering ruderalis subspecies has become more common.

As any cannabis gardener knows, a main aspect of cannabis cultivation with sativa and indica strains is flower forcing. Normally plants must be forced to enter flowering, which means to begin forming buds. This is accomplished by changing the light cycle so that plants get 10–12 hours of uninterrupted darkness. This light cycle mimics outdoor conditions, since days get longer (and the night darkness shorter) until the summer solstice on June 22, after which the days shorten through the remainder of the summer and fall. The difference in light-hours from summer to winter depends in part on latitude. Close to the equator, both weather and light-hours vary less from summer to winter. The differences in both light hours and seasonal weather are more dramatic as one moves north or south in latitude.

Until recently, gardeners had to plan for the dark period carefully. For outdoor growers, this meant selecting varieties that would be forced to flower early enough to finish in their location, or to plan to block light to outdoor plants using covering. Indoor gardeners needed to ensure the room had no light leaks and plan garden tending around the light cycle. While these are still good measures to take, autoflowering varieties reduce the requirements to strictly control the light and dark cycles.

Autoflowering strains instead take their cue to flower based on how long they have been growing rather than how much uninterrupted darkness they receive. Autoflowering varieties bring a new versatility to growing, allowing plants to flourish in environments where light pollution would have created difficulties. They also make plants a little easier for new growers who do not have to master the light regimen or monitor it strictly in order to grow a successful crop.

SOG This icon is listed only on plants suitable for sea of green gardens. Plants in these gardens are spaced together very closely so that each plant needs to grow little if any to fill the canopy. Plants are forced to flower soon after they are placed in the flowering space. Eliminating the vegetative growth stage decreases turnaround. SOG gardens hold 3 to 6 plants per square foot.

This icon is listed only on plants suitable for screen of green gardens. There are many different versions of screen of green, or SCROG. The one thing these methods have in common is that they use a screen to support buds, allowing for denser bud growth. This can be done both horizontally and vertically. This situation often happens when plants of different varieties are being cultivated. The problem with this technique is that while the topside of the buds receives plenty of light, the undersides do not. See the screen of green by Franco on page 22 for more information.

Once again, fuller descriptions are found within the descriptive text for each variety. The icons are fast reference points. They give you an idea of where the story is going. The accompanying variety description provides more nuanced details and tips about the plant's preferences. Still, we have to admit that we love the photos the most. They show what words can only attempt to express. I'm sure they will provide you with hours of sightseeing pleasure.

Quick Key to Icons

English • En Español • Deutsch
En Français • Italiano • Nederlands

Strain Type

S
Sativa

I
Indica

IS
Indica/Sativa

SI
Sativa/Indica

SR
Sativa/Ruderalis

IR
Indica/Ruderalis

SIR
Sativa/Indica/Ruderalis

Feminized

Autoflowering

Growing Info

Flowering Time
Tiempo de floración
Blütezeit
Durée de floraison
Stagione della fioritura
Bloetijd

Parentage
Genética
Mutterpflanze
Descendance
Genitori
Stamboom

Yield
Rendimiento
Ertag
Rendement
Raccolta
Opbrengst

SOG
Sea of Green

Screen of Green

Indoor
Interior
Drinnen
D´Intérieur
Dentro
Binnen

Outdoor
Exterior
Draussen
d´Extérieur
Fuori
Buiten

Indoor/Outdoor
Interior/Exterior
Drinnen/Draussen
d´Intérieur/d´Extérieur
Dentro/Fuori
Binnen/Buiten

Sensory Experience

Buzz
Efecto
die Art des Turns
Effets
Effetti
High Effekt

Taste/Smell
Sabor/Aroma
Geschmack/Geruch
Saveur/Arôme
Sapore/Odore
Smaak/Geua

Breeder Location

Canada

Netherlands

Spain

United Kingdom

U.S.A.

Alaskan Ice • AMS • Anesthesia • Angelma[t]

Blue Cheese • Barney's Farm G13-Haze

Haze • Carnival • Cataract Kush • CH9 Fl

• Chiesel • Cocoa Kush • Crippled Pit

Dark Star • DelaHaze • Diabolic Funxta

Haze • Easy Rider • Funxta'z Purple Ca

Headband • Herijuana • Himalaya Gold

#5 • Jamaican Pearl • Jock Horror • K-Tra

• L.A.P.D. • Lemon Skunk • LSD • Man

Morning Star • Mr. Nice • Northern Light

• Pit Bull • PolarLight • Purple Voodo

• Skunk Haze • Sleestack • Smoothie •

Southern Nights • Super Lemon Haze •

Kali • The OG #18 • The Ultimate • Titan

• Urban Poison • Vanilla Kush Vanillu

• Apollo 13BX • Automaria • Barney's Farm Black Berry • Bubble Cheese • Buddha er • CH9 G Bolt • CH9 Jack 33 • Cheesus Critical #47 • Crystalberry • Dancehall Dr. Grinspoon • Dready Kush • Dutch Kush • G-Bomb • Green House Thai • ranian Autoflower • Jack F6 • Jack Flash • Kandahar • Killing Fields • Kushadelic la #1 • Mekong High • Morning Glory • Apollo G13 • NYPD • Oregon Pinot Noir Qleaner • Querkle • Raspberry Cough nowStorm • Soma-licious • Somantra • viss Cheese • Tahoe Gold • Taiga • The Haze • Tora Bora • Tropi-canna • Tundra • Veryberry • Vortex • Whitaker Blues

Varieties

Alaskan Ice

Green House Seed Company

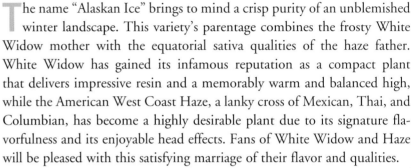

The name "Alaskan Ice" brings to mind a crisp purity of an unblemished winter landscape. This variety's parentage combines the frosty White Widow mother with the equatorial sativa qualities of the haze father. White Widow has gained its infamous reputation as a compact plant that delivers impressive resin and a memorably warm and balanced high, while the American West Coast Haze, a lanky cross of Mexican, Thai, and Columbian, has become a highly desirable plant due to its signature flavorfulness and its enjoyable head effects. Fans of White Widow and Haze will be pleased with this satisfying marriage of their flavor and qualities.

Alaskan Ice blends its parental qualities to deliver a balanced mix of sativa and indica. This variety creeps up gently like a glacier and delivers an alert, euphoric mental feeling that balances relaxation and energy, resonating throughout the body. Gardeners will find this plant is good for indoor or outdoor environments. Indoors, it is better suited to a screen of green rather than a sea of green setup since the haze parentage comes through, encouraging a branchy plant that grows quickly during vegetation and requires some management to keep the branches orderly and focused on flower power. This plant prefers a strong EC, up to 2.0, and will grow to be about 5 feet (150 cm) indoors. It can reach heights of 9–10 feet (300 cm) when grown outdoors under natural light. The 9-week flowering phase makes this plant suitable to outdoor grows only in regions where a long season of temperate daylight is a reasonable expectation—at least until late October in the western hemisphere. Mature plants will have a frost of Alaskan ice coating the branches in a resinous tundra-like sparkle.

This variety has a very spicy aroma, leading with black pepper and cedar flavors, and followed by an aftertaste of incense and forest moss. On first puff, it can be slightly acrid but soon mellows into a fresh herbal-sandalwood flavor that is pleasant to the palate. This is a variety to share at parties and on joyous occasions. It is not well suited for a daytime or solitary smoke, or for intense focus and in-the-zone productivity. As medicine, Alaskan Ice has been promising for treating pain, glaucoma, and depression, and stimulating appetite.

70/30

alert, euphoric, energetic, uplifting

sour/spicy sandalwood herbal haze

60–65 days

♀White Widow x ♂haze

750–1000g per plant out

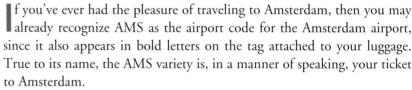

AMS

Green House Seed Company

If you've ever had the pleasure of traveling to Amsterdam, then you may already recognize AMS as the airport code for the Amsterdam airport, since it also appears in bold letters on the tag attached to your luggage. True to its name, the AMS variety is, in a manner of speaking, your ticket to Amsterdam.

Amsterdam is an international city, and its Dutch namesake variety has done a little country hopping itself. The AMS mom is a Swiss indica strain named Fragolina, the Italian name for strawberries. The dad, also of Swiss origin with an Italian name, is a sativa called Gran Flora, meaning "great plants." When brought together in Amsterdam as AMS, the cross leans toward indica, with the trademark body high from the indica side of the cannabis family, balanced by a blissful sativa cerebral effect.

AMS is a multi-branch plant originally developed with outdoor growing in mind. It makes a great mountain plant, thriving in cold-night climates. AMS will also thrive indoors, but requires more tending. This variety is not suited for sea of green methods. She grows a bit tall and stretchy, and her size requires attentiveness to produce manageable plants in an indoor space. AMS fares well when allowed to develop its strong pine-tree shape of strong branches from which to dangle its enticing flowery fruit. This plant likes organics and soil based growing and takes 8–9 weeks from flower forcing. In the great outdoors, it requires a growing season that lasts through the end of October before hitting a cold snap. Mature plants can easily hit 8 feet (2.4 meters) in an outdoor grow, but the average indoor height ranges from 4 to 5 feet (120–250 cm).

These plants hint at what is to come when, as they approach ripeness, they begin to saturate the air with their intensely sweet smell. The aroma of the cured buds is predominantly fruity, maintaining strawberry qualities from the mother and adding hints of peach or plum. These buds also have a hint of sour citrus that resembles the tang of grapefruit or blood orange. The aroma translates very well to the after-burned flavor. Friends who favor the fruity varieties will perk up when they get a whiff of this variety at any stage from baggie to smoke.

The AMS high is gradual. It spreads slowly within the body, heightening until it reaches its apex, then dissipating rather quickly. The body effect is smooth and relaxing with a deep muscle effect, making it a successful choice for multiple sclerosis or insomnia. AMS is a smoke for winding down and kicking back rather than kicking off the party mood. To maximize the enjoyment of this strain, have a nice toke before a massage, or take a puff from the vantage point of a lounge chair on the deck after the week's work is done.

 70/30

 social, heady, blissful, playful

 strawberry, caramel, tobacco

 50–60 days

 ♀Swiss indica x ♂Swiss sativa

 750–1000g per plant out

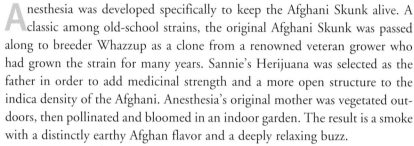

Anesthesia
Sannie's Seeds

Anesthesia was developed specifically to keep the Afghani Skunk alive. A classic among old-school strains, the original Afghani Skunk was passed along to breeder Whazzup as a clone from a renowned veteran grower who had grown the strain for many years. Sannie's Herijuana was selected as the father in order to add medicinal strength and a more open structure to the indica density of the Afghani. Anesthesia's original mother was vegetated outdoors, then pollinated and bloomed in an indoor garden. The result is a smoke with a distinctly earthy Afghan flavor and a deeply relaxing buzz.

Anesthesia starts as a low branchy plant with broad indica leaves. When grown from seed, these plants branch extensively and yield better with ample space, but they still tend to form one large dense main cola. Anesthesia prefers a calcium-rich substrate, but all growing techniques and media are okay. In a sea of green method, gardeners should plant no more than nine plants per square meter. It is also great for screen of green gardens due to the branching and open structure. This wide plant needs generous floor space to reach its full potential. Whazzup recommends 4–5 plants per square meter when grown as multi-branch plants from cuttings. Anesthesia shows gender relatively late. As she enters flowering, the growth speeds up, and she doubles in size, reaching between 3.5 and 4 feet (1 meter) in height.

At maturity, the plants begin to use less water, the deep green leaves start to yellow, and the buds develop red-brown pistils. Trichomes form a thick carpet on the leaves and buds. They do not all need to be milky to be harvest-ready. Though predominantly indica, the open plant structure and the low leaf ratio makes Anesthesia easy to trim. The Herijuana-dominant phenotypes finish first and are also the most compact and most resinous. A separate mixed phenotype finishes a little slower and has the best combination of dark musky taste and potency. Don't let the modest size of the colas mislead you—their dense chunkiness means they weigh in heavy and explode in the grinder. Since these plants have a tight bud structure, it is best to avoid high humidity during the last weeks of flowering.

Anesthesia is named for the narcotic, body stone that its smoke induces. By definition, "anesthesia" is a state in which awareness of pain or discomfort in the body is reduced, and a relaxing or sedative effect is created. The Anesthesia variety causes a deep physical mellowing that slowly works through one's limbs like a warm blanket, while allowing the mind to stay engaged. As a medicinal strength strain, it may be too potent to be enjoyable for beginners or casual recreational smokers. However, patients who rely on indica body effects but want to stay mentally alert will enjoy the balance of these qualities. The old-school taste is earthy and dark, with a hint of coffee tones that will appeal to fans of deep hashy flavors.

relaxed, stoned, sedated

Afghani, earthy, coffee

64–70 days

♀Positronics Afghan/Skunk x ♂Herijuana

450–500g per m²

SOG

Sannie's Seeds Breeder's Choice Selection: Anesthesia

Sannie's Seeds is a small Dutch company that features varieties lovingly bred by the owner Sannie. However, Sannie has also developed a line of "Breeder's Choice" varieties. These strains are selected from the work of a close-knit group of specialized breeders. Sannie selects Breeder's Choice varieties based on their unique contributions to desired traits and qualities. This allows the work of dedicated specialty breeders to be shared with the larger cannabis community.

One of these breeders is Whazzup. Whazzup has dedicated his breeding efforts to developing Anesthesia, the medical strength strain based on the original 1980s Positronics Afghan Skunk and the modern Herijuana. Here he talks about how he became involved in this project:

"The first time I planted a seed was back in 1983. It was bag seed that I planted in dirt, and I can't even remember its origins, but the plants became huge! I quickly learned about males and females the hard way. By 2005, it had been years since I had grown cannabis, but I was inspired by the Overgrow and Hennepdesk Internet forums to learn about the latest developments and start up again.

"I did a lot of research, focusing on organic nutrients, to master the organic way of growing. I experimented with different light sources and combinations of metal halide (MH) and high-pressure sodium (HPS) lighting. As I got more involved, I began to meet medical marijuana patients, and this increased my interest in the effect of specific strains. I would donate part of every harvest to the patients and ask them for feedback. When I was confident that I had mastered the latest techniques for organic growing, I made my first crosses, starting with Anesthesia in 2007 and 2008. After the success of field tests, Anesthesia became available as a Breeder's Choice through Sannie's shop and has been a medical favorite in Holland since that time.

"When I breed, I prefer to grow my plants in a screen of green setup. The even lighting of all the buds guarantees the highest percentage of good seeds. SCROGGing creates a sort of intimacy between you and your plants. You learn to pay attention to every branch, every bend, every bud, and every growing characteristic of the individual plants. It is a great way to become familiar with a strain.

"Mycorrhizae and beneficial bacteria should be on any organic grower's menu! My favorite single organic nutrients are (clean cane) molasses, kelp, and humic acid. My advice is: Don't overcomplicate your nutrients! Always understand first why you are giving a nutrient before actually doing it."

Angelmatic
Ministry of Cannabis

There has been a quest in recent years to tease out the autoflowering characteristic from the Russian-born ruderalis variant of cannabis. Autoflowering liberates growers from a strict light schedule; however, ruderalis has a reputation for otherwise mediocre qualities. The artful breeder must coax out the autoflowering trait while maintaining the connoisseur elements from the sativa and indica strains. Ministry of Cannabis began their quest for a high quality autoflowering plant with the Little Angel variety. They have continued this program with the Angelmatic strain, an evolution of Little Angel. Angelmatic improves on the stability and size of its ruderalis-cross predecessor, with a slightly larger size and better harvest. Ruderalis has been crossed into both sides of Angelmatic's family tree. The mother is a sativa-indica-ruderalis hybrid with sativa dominance from regions in south Russia and Europe. The father is also a three-way hybrid, but is half-indica. The resulting cross is a bonsai strain that autoflowers and finishes from seed to harvest in roughly 60 days.

Angelmatic is compact with light green cone buds dressed in frosty white resin. The leaves are medium green with a structure that balances the hybrid influences. This plant has moderate branching that extends in a vertical rather than horizontal direction. Angelmatic's main stem is generally double the size of the side branches, lending itself to a sea of green approach. It can be pruned to the main branch and deliver good chunky buds from its sturdy stem.

As a fast growing, compact plant, Angelmatic has vitality and shows resistance to pests that will be appreciated indoors or out. Ministry recommends cultivating Angelmatic in soil with a generous supplement of nitrogen in its feeding regimen. Outdoors, this plant still prefers a temperate climate. With good light and normal temperatures, the buds form well, but if basic growing conditions aren't met, these dwarf-sized plants will produce buds that are skimpy and loose, reducing yields. Each plant can produce about an ounce indoors and two ounces outdoors, with possible yields up to 3.5 ounces (100 grams) in full summer with a temperate climate.

The Angelmatic aroma is a sweet mix of flowers and candy, and the flavor follows suit but adds a nice contrast of sourness in the aftertaste. The effect is active and friendly, and comes on slowly, taking a few minutes to fully register. This is a social high, better for mellow activities than focused concentration. Enjoy it with others over dinner, games, or just hanging out.

 40/30/30

 active, social, energetic

 sour bubblegum candy

 42–45 days

 ♀sativa-dominant ruderalis hybrid x ♂indica-dominant ruderalis hybrid

 50g per plant in 100g per plant out

8

Apollo 13BX
TGA Seeds

A pollo 13BX is a West Coast strain that brings together some cannabis from the outer stratosphere. The mother is an Apollo 13 F1, and the father is a strain called Vortex, a cross between Space Queen and Apollo 13X.

This sativa-dominant variety can be grown outside if the weather remains plant friendly through the end of October. Apollo 13BX also lives happily indoors, where it grows in a vine-like structure that is cooperative in either a screen of green or sea of green system. It can also be grown into large bushy plants so long as the stems are supported. The gardener will need to decide how to tame these plants to best suit the grow space. Apollo 13BX is an agreeable, non-fussy plant, but in order to reach her true yield potential, she needs to be topped and trained. After she is topped, Apollo 13BX likes to grow sideways and can get quite wide. If space is a concern, this flexible plant can be trained to grow vertically using bamboo stakes. The average Apollo 13BX finishes after flowering for 8 weeks.

This plant is a moderate feeder that does not like heavy nutrients but thrives when given a healthy boost in nitrogen. The bud development is almost pod-like, forming long pointy colas at its many budding sites, with the lower buds getting chunkier and more spear-shaped. Apollo 13BX clones well, but the long thin colas take a little extra trim time at harvest.

Apollo 13BX is the type of strain that earns marijuana nicknames like "the fruit." When cured these lime-green buds have a heavy dank smell of overripe fruit, a mixture of rich sultry mangoes and acidic lemons and an underlying pepper tickle that comes through in the aftertaste. This is a motivational strain. With just a few hits, many people are inspired to get stuff done, whether writing, cleaning, working in the yard, taking photos, or getting out on a hike in the great outdoors. It is an up, happy yet purposeful high that invigorates as well as a cup of good coffee. When used in baked goods, it offers effective pain relief without inducing a nap. The bubble hash it produces makes some growers dream of converting their entire crop.

 85/15

 creative, energizing

 overripe fruit, mango, pepper

 56 days

 ♀Apollo 13 F1 x ♂Vortex

 medium

 SOG

Breeding Apollo 13BX
Subcool
TGA Seeds

The Apollo 13BX strain represents thousands of hours of selective breeding. The THC profile of Apollo 13 has been an inspiration to TGA Seeds because it provides such a pleasant stimulation to one's mental and creative energy.

This is our first available backcross of the Apollo 13. When creating the Apollo 13BX strain, the male was the key. We took painstaking care in selecting the male, spending over a year on research and ultimately examining 60 potential plants before identifying the stable cross that exhibited all of the desirable characteristics we were seeking.

The Apollo 13BX stands out for its instant and powerful motivational buzz. We really wanted a strain that kept the Apollo 13 "high" intact rather than drifting to a more stoned experience. It is a clear and expansive cerebral high but is not speedy or prone to paranoia. This variety defies all stereotypes of the cannabis couch potato. Instead, Apollo 13BX is a get-up-and-go strain that offers a boost of mental inspiration to the diverse community of creative, intelligent, and active people out there who enjoy the spark that cannabis can add to whatever art, music, writing, or other project they are undertaking. This strain highlights the positive qualities that marijuana has to offer humankind because it wakes up the expansive and euphoric tendencies that we each possess.

11

Automaria

Paradise Seeds

 body stone

 spicy floral

 55–65 days

 Kazakhstan ruderalis x̄ Afghani indica

 350g per m²

 SOG

Automaria is the latest ruderalis hybrid strain from Paradise Seeds. This variety combines the desired autoflowering quality from cannabis ruderalis with the more dense, savory, and pleasant cannabinoid balance of a hardy landrace Afghan indica. The ruderalis strain in the Paradise breeding program comes from Kazakhstan, a former republic in the Soviet Union. Kazakhstan is the largest landlocked country in the world, with an area roughly the size of Western Europe, but a sparse population with a density about 5% of Europe. It is a vast, flat steppe that stretches between the oases and deserts of central Asia to ruderalis' Russian home.

Generally speaking, ruderalis is miniature compared with its indica and sativa siblings. For this reason, many ruderalis-cross plants not only autoflower, but also have a short flowering cycle, maturing quickly into dark and compact plants. Automaria is no exception. This plant maintains a smaller stature than most indicas, and because it has a fast cycle and is free from forcing, it is possible to complete two or three harvests in a spring-to-fall outdoor season.

Indoors, this plant performs equally well in hydro or soil systems. Flowering starts soon after growth is established. If larger plants are desired, transplanting them during the third week will boost the size. Automaria finishes from seed in 8 weeks, with decent yields for such small and fast-flowering plants. While this may not be a top choice for those with ideal conditions, Automaria is a good selection for gardeners who want smaller plants that flower regardless of light exposure and have a rapid cycle. Automaria's qualities make for a stealthy plant that can succeed in situations where other plants would be ill-suited.

Automaria buds are stoney little nuggets with a pleasant sheen of resin. This strain's flavor has some Afghan indica spice, but keeps a fragrant floral edge. The Automaria buzz centralizes in the core of the body, and then emanates throughout for a mellow enjoyment.

Barney's Farm Blue Cheese
Barney's Farm

Barney's Farm Blue Cheese crosses the popular UK Cheese strain with the perennially popular Blueberry. Cheese is thought to be a distinctive Skunk #1 variant known for its pungent, intense flavors as much as for its immensely enjoyable and easygoing buzz. This strain came up in the UK, where it got a reputation as kind bud, but was only available in clone form. Then Big Buddha backcrossed it in the mid-2000s to create seeds, which opened up breeding possibilities. Here, Cheese is crossed with an indica-dominant Blueberry father, a strain known for its flavors and its purple-blue coloration.

When selectively crossed, these two distinct tasting and widely recognized varieties have resulted in an incredibly fragrant and easy to grow strain. Barney's Farm Blue Cheese likes to shoot up long and straight, forming a thick main stem. The side branching is significant and forms a strong tree-like frame that can be easily trained to a screen of green. This plant stays short and stocky, finishing in 9–10 weeks with highly productive yields of tight, sticky spear-shaped colas. Buds are light green and springy to the touch, with pale orange hairs jutting out of elongated calyxes. Average yields are 1.5–2 ounces (45–60g) per plant.

Barney's Farm Blue Cheese is a variety with a one-of-a-kind taste—it is rich, round, and smooth, with a connoisseur's spectrum from the sweet and floral to the deep, earthen chocolate baseline. The intense and pungent earthy musk aromas of the Cheese are retained, but are now tempered with sweet incense-like Blueberry notes. The Barney's Farm Blue Cheese high is very heady. It creeps up then comes on strong and indica, with a full body stone. Many people will enjoy the trajectory of this mentally peaceful and physically relieving buzz. It has a pleasant entry and exit, although as it winds down, some people might find it a bit of a knockout, requiring a short nap to reset before moving on to any other activity.

I

 calm, relaxing

 berries and cream

 60–70 days

 ♀Skunk #1 Cheese variant x ♂Blueberry

 45-60g per plant in

 in preferred

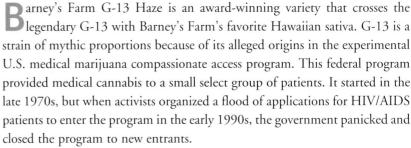

Barney's Farm G13-Haze
Barney's Farm

 S I

 soaring, cerebral

 fruity haze

 70–80 days

 G-13 x Hawaiian sativa

 500g per m²

 in preferred

 SOG

Barney's Farm G-13 Haze is an award-winning variety that crosses the legendary G-13 with Barney's Farm's favorite Hawaiian sativa. G-13 is a strain of mythic proportions because of its alleged origins in the experimental U.S. medical marijuana compassionate access program. This federal program provided medical cannabis to a small select group of patients. It started in the late 1970s, but when activists organized a flood of applications for HIV/AIDS patients to enter the program in the early 1990s, the government panicked and closed the program to new entrants.

Some have said that any government-grown weed could only be low-grade, but others insist that the government program's scientific approach resulted in the creation of a superstrain: G-13. Rumors circulated in the 1990s claiming that a G-13 clone had been smuggled from the grow facility. Shortly thereafter breeders had backcrossed the G-13 into seed form and the name began to crop up all over the map. In the Barney's Farm cross, G-13 has been combined with a great tasting island sativa that has strong haze influences in composition. Straight out of the gate, Barney's Farm G-13 Haze has a very nice smell of ripe fruit and haze-sandalwood spiciness.

This variety is best compared with other sativa-dominant and haze plants. In general, haze hybrids require the vegetative time to be kept short. Flower forcing for this variety is recommended as soon as the clones have had a chance to establish themselves, which is helpful given that flowering times are fairly long, taking 10–12 weeks to ripen.

When vegged as directed, Barney's Farm G-13 Haze maintains a medium-tall stature with sturdy branches. This plant grows vigorously, and the flower structure has better density than many hazes, resulting in an above-average yield. The size and sturdiness of the plants also make it easier to grow in restricted indoor spaces than the typical haze. The buds have a bit of sativa sponginess to them, but this plant likes to form one large main cola on the central branch. This tendency makes it ideal for a SOG garden, although SCROG is another good choice. Not only does G-13 Haze offer healthy yields with good THC levels, it also possesses intense aromas and flavors and a powerful cerebral smoke worth savoring. This variety encapsulates the winning qualities of flavor and high that many sativa lovers seek out, but maintains a bass note of indica that anchors the effects nicely. Barney's Farm G-13 Haze has had multiple wins at the High Times Cannabis Cup, taking 2nd place in 2006, and 1st place in 2007.

Black Berry

Nirvana

These days, everyone has their BlackBerry® to stay connected and functional in the modern world. Nirvana believes their version of Black Berry may help you deal with the pace of the modern world in a different sense. The Black Berry variety actually gets its name from a combination of its parents' names; it is a Black Domino/Raspberry Cough hybrid. The Black Domino mother is an indica-dominant hybrid that originated in the Seattle area, then traveled to Amsterdam in clone form. In this cross, she is combined with Raspberry Cough (also in this book), an indica-sativa hybrid of Nirvana's ICE strain, and a landrace strain from Cambodia.

Black Berry likes a steady, stable home that is kept within ideal parameters. Because this plant is exacting, results will be largely based on the gardener's ability to maintain conditions, making it more suitable to an experienced hand and an established gardening setup. Black Berry is best as an indoor plant due to its sensitivity to weather variation and its flowering time, which ranges from 9 to 11 weeks depending on the phenotype. Indoor environments are the only suitable places for this plant outside the equatorial region, but inside that geographic area, it can thrive outdoors and will finish by the middle or end of October.

Black Berry retains her Black Domino mother's figure, forming a tight, almost prim narrow plant structure that is branchier for some phenotypes. Growth is uniform and compact, and turns dark velvety green. This strain performs best in soil, but flourishes in many setups, including sea of green arrangements or as multi-branch plants. The Black Berry bud development is also tight, forming long pointy, or in some cases, bulb-shaped colas with minimal hairs. Despite the density of the buds, Black Berry is resistant to molds. It is also a very stinky grower. Using organics helps to bring out the best flavor and aroma. By finish, Black Berry roughly doubles in size and averages yields of 400–500 grams per square meter in a sea of green with 600-watt lights.

The Black Berry high is upbeat and clear, with a quick onset and a nice tapering endurance. It is a functional smoke well suited to daytime activities and can create a more casual unhurried sense of well-being without impairing one beyond comfort in most social situations. The flavor is heavy and fuel-like and forms thick smoke. The finish leaves hints of spicy South Asian flavor on the tongue. Black Berry was released in 2009, and has gained fast popularity among patients in Canada.

 60/40

 talkative, even head/body

 spicy, acrid, Asian sativa

 55–65 days

 ♀Black Domino x ♂Raspberry Cough

 400–500g per m2

 SOG

Bubble Cheese
Big Buddha Seeds

 85/15

 sedative, sensual, stoney

 bubblegum, kush

 55–65 days

 Bubblegum x ♀Cheese x ♂reversed Hubba Bubba Kush

 200g per plant

 SOG

Big Buddha has been spreading the gospel of Cheese throughout the UK. In this mission, he finds a flock of Cheeseheads wherever he goes, and comes across many different versions or phenotypes of the Cheese variety, as well as seeing many Cheese crosses. One unique variation came from a friend who is affectionately nicknamed Mr. Cheese. Mr. Cheese provided the mother for what has become the Bubble Cheese. The mother was a cutting that crossed a UK Bubblegum strain with OG Cheese (Exodus). This mother was similar in growth and appearance to the original Cheese but had a much more pronounced bubblegum flavor. Big Buddha created a "father" from a "reversed" Hubba Bubba Kush from Amsterdam. In other words, Hubba Bubba Kush was induced to create pollen on a female plant in order to feminize this strain.

Bubble Cheese is a mostly indica hybrid that grows into a solid Kush-like indica plant—compact and dense, with dark green fat squatty leaves. Its branching is short, thick, and minimal, making it a good performer in a sea of green setup. Bubble Cheese is a moderate to heavy feeder who takes 8–10 weeks to finish. It is recommended for indoor gardens, but if outdoor weather stays above freezing through early November, count yourself among the lucky few who can cultivate a Bubble Cheese garden outdoors.

Expert growers or resourceful beginners with a green thumb will produce some pungent indica with this strain. Indoors, the Bubble Cheese can reach heights of up to 7 feet and produces only moderate yields, averaging 200 grams per plant. The buds are compact nuggets of chewing-gum bud, sticky sweet with resin. The yield can be supplemented by turning Bubble Cheese trimmings into hubbly bubbly hash goodness. The fat glands are there, waiting to be collected, and will not disappoint in quantity or quality.

Mixing bubblegum with cheese may not sound so delicious—until you remember that Cheese doesn't taste like, well, cheese. Cheese is the old-school spicy-sweet Kush. It possesses an aroma and flavor that when cured correctly brings back wistful memories of the primo tastes of yesteryear. This is Kush with some sugar sprinkled on top; sweet-tooth Kush fans will be very happy. The Bubble Cheese high comes on strong. Its sedating buzz has a down-tempo, sleepy bodily sensation. It is not a mental downer, but brings a positivity that allows one to wander pleasantly while listening to music or drift off into dreamland. As a medicinal aid, it is especially appropriate for insomnia or muscle pain.

Buddha Haze
Big Buddha Seeds

Photos: Bud the Cheese 420

While living in Amsterdam, Big Buddha breeders managed to acquire many different clones for personal headstash. One of these was an amazing pheno of Amnesia Haze. This specific cutting was a Bubblegum phenotype that descended from two previous Cannabis Cup winners. The mother was an Amsterdam coffeeshop clone related to three great hazes: Super Silver Haze, Amnesia Haze, and G-13 Haze. Big Buddha took this haze pheno to Spain, where oops—she got knocked up with the feminized pollen of a Manga Rosa plant, a landrace strain acquired by friends when they traveled through Brazil.

The happy accident of this cross produced a beautiful baby girl, the Buddha Haze. This is a haze treat befitting the Buddha in everyone. She has a unique taste blending mango haze with pure sativa tones in a way that is usually found only in South America. From the start, the Buddha Haze is an attractive plant with elegant sativa-slender leaves. The haze structure has loose branching and forms heavy flower tops that benefit from supports. Indoor gardeners should flower this plant soon after establishing vegetation, since haze sativas really do like to stretch out. Given the super long 10–14 week season she requires, most Buddha Haze growers will probably be gardening indoors.

Like all haze-dominant plants, the Buddha Haze requires a gardener who is devoted, attentive, and knowledgeable. This pretty gal is a fussy plant who has particular tastes. The more experienced sativa or haze gardener will fare better with this variety. Buddha Haze eats light and does not like too many nutrients. She will cooperate in both hydro and soil systems and prefers things warmer, thriving in slightly hot environments and showing her displeasure when the room gets too chilly.

Buddha Haze's light green calyxes form compact bunches along the branches, growing long tendrils that turn copper as they mature. The smell of haze is strong in the garden air. This is one of the sweeter tasting hazes out there, mixing the pungent sweet fruit flavors with a mango edge and a hint of sweet bubblegum candy. The Buddha Haze high has no ceiling—the sky is the limit. The strong and seamless beginning builds in a long euphoric rush, making Buddha Haze good for parties or festivities of all kinds. The buzz creates a very functional state because it keeps an alert, electric, and cheerful vibe that inspires thought without causing one's mind to wander off.

 S I 85/15

 hazy, trippy, giggly, happy

 candy, mango, fruity, haze

 75–90 days

 ♀Amnesia Haze x ♂Manga Rosa

 100g per plant

Carnival
Ministry of Cannabis

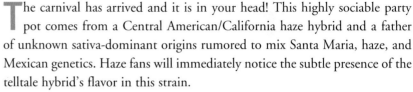

The carnival has arrived and it is in your head! This highly sociable party pot comes from a Central American/California haze hybrid and a father of unknown sativa-dominant origins rumored to mix Santa Maria, haze, and Mexican genetics. Haze fans will immediately notice the subtle presence of the telltale hybrid's flavor in this strain.

Carnival is no Christmas tree, and she does not stretch like many of her haze-dominant cousins. Rather than bushing out, this plant extends growth upward. Branching is only moderate and of an average length, making her a natural volunteer for sea of green methods. If Carnival is grown as a multi-branch plant, Ministry recommends topping the plants for optimal yields. This plant cooperates in hydro and soil media, and shows good resistance to both molds and parasites. The flowering time is 9 weeks or the beginning of October if started outside in the second half of July. Carnival prefers slightly warm rooms over cold, and when grown outdoors, she does better in climates that stay warmer or don't dip too far into the cold range.

Carnival buds are compact and glossy with a white sheen masking a pale and tropical green interior. The leaves are moderately thick and range from light to dark green. Carnival's smell stays light and fresh, so the grow room is never too dank. Although this plant is not too difficult to grow, it is not ideal for the beginner and benefits from a more experienced hand. At finish, this plant averages a height of about 5 feet (150 cm). In hydro systems, a gram per watt is possible.

True to her name, Carnival is vibrant with flavor elements that are fresh and enticing, ranging from a sugary dry grape to aloe, lemon, and haze. One whiff and many connoisseurs will eagerly line up with tickets for the promise of a euphoric ride. Carnival enters the senses quickly and creates a lucid and humorous merrymaking mood, although it may make an already anxious person hyperactive. Carnivals are events designed to release pent up energies, celebrate life, and forget about the workaday world for a while. Soak up the vividness that this strain adds to everyday surroundings.

 80/20

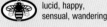 lucid, happy, sensual, wandering

 fresh citrus haze

 63 days

 ♀ haze x ♂ hybrid

 450g per m² in 300g per plant out

 SOG

What is the SCREEN OF GREEN (SCROG) Growing Method?

By Franco
Green House Seed Company

The SCROG system is the practical application of a very simple concept: a screen, or net, is placed horizontally over the plants during vegetative growth, and the plants themselves are allowed to stretch through the screen toward the light. The screen can be used in several ways. Sometimes branches are tied to the screen to form a flat surface under the lights. At other times the screen simply serves a support function for the vertically stretching branches and later for the buds. The benefits for the grower derive from the versatility of the system. The height at which the screen is placed depends on many factors, including the desired crop height, the plants' genetic predisposition to height, and the intended length of the vegetative growth period. The screen is usually made of nylon netting or a rigid grid, and it has open squares ranging in size from 4 to 12 inches (10-30 cm). The larger the openings, the less support the plants will get. On average, SCROG demands less plants per square meter compared to SOG, and it is especially useful for a setup in which only a few large branchy plants are being grown in a confined space.

SCROG in a Grow-Box Setup

When the SCROG is applied in a grow-box context, it is usually to flatten the canopy and to form a solid, well supported layer of flowers, one that can be kept at the desired distance from the lamps without risk of overstretch and burning. When approaching SCROG in a

SCROG keeps each bud growing straight up, within its own section of the canopy.

A rigid frame was placed over these plants to spread out the branches.

grow-box, it is important to consider a few determining factors: the heat threat, the absence of light under the screen, and the different needs in plant nutrition that this system requires.

Heat is always an issue in a grow-box system. The reality is that most grow-box producers for the commercial market are more concerned with security and discretion than with plant health and well being. As a result, most grow-box systems lack proper ventilation in favor of a quiet, stealthy setup. When SCROG is applied to a confined space, it is important to realize that there will be two completely different climate areas inside the grow-box: an "over-the-screen" climate and an "under-the-screen" climate. The temperature over the screen will be much higher, and that's where the hot air should be vigorously pumped out on a constant-flow basis. Fresh air should be pulled in from under the screen, so that it travels through the canopy to reach the exhaust fan.

Looking up at the screen.

Another issue to monitor is the near-absence of light under the screen. It is recommended to trim any small branches and leaves that don't receive enough light so that they stay green and healthy. Getting rid of these weak, penalized parts of the plants will improve the general well being of the canopy, thus reducing stress and increasing production.

Finally, the feeding needs of the plants have to be considered. When plants grow long and stretchy side branches, they benefit from extra N and P during the first weeks of flowering. This is especially important when growing sativas. Moreover, longer branches and a hot canopy demand more water and will need water at shorter intervals. The size of containers has to be large enough to allow plants to grow into and over the screen without sacrificing the pace of new growth.

Other SCROG Set-ups

Screen of green can also be successfully applied to very different situations, such as growing really tall plants indoors. When vertical space is not an issue, maximal production is achieved by exploiting the height of the plants. This is particularly true when growing sativas. In order to grow very tall plants without the problem of branches bending during heavy cola formation, a single or multiple SCROG can be applied. In a multiple SCROG, plants are allowed to grow through more than one layer of screen so that they are supported at different set heights. Usually 2 or 3 screens do the job. They are placed at 1- to 2-foot (30-60 cm) intervals. The plants grow through the screens, and when they reach the top screen they are tightened to form a flat canopy. This system requires additional lateral light since the stages of growth between the first and last screens have to receive adequate light to avoid stress and lack of productivity.

Whether using one screen or multiple screens, once the system is in place and the plants are growing through a screen, it should not be moved again. This means that the growroom has to be set up to allow watering and maintenance without any need for moving or altering the screen position. If the screen covers a large area, an automatic watering system is usually the best option, unless the plants are very tall and the screen is placed high enough that walking under it is possible. As for the grow-box setup, it is convenient to trim the lower branches since they cannot receive good light.

Overall, SCROG is not a system that can, or should, be viewed as static. The only stationary part is the position of the screen itself. All other factors must be flexible to guarantee the best results. SCROG should be seen as a way to improve an already tested growroom or grow-box. If, for example, one tries to grow really tall sativas, but has falling branches and broken buds as a result, SCROG is a good solution. Besides being inexpensive, easy to use, and easy to dismantle, SCROG is always a fun experiment. At harvest, the screen can be recycled as a plant hanger during the drying process, a true expression of its flexible nature.

For more by Franco, see:
www.myspace.com/francogreenhouse

Netting was stretched across a wide area in this greenhouse to support the buds as they grew through it.

Cataract Kush

DNA Genetics

 I

 creeper, strong indica stone

 hashy, sweet spice, pungent

 56–63 days

 ♀ OG Kush x ♂ LA Confidential

 average 350–500g per m²

 SOG

Cataract Kush is a full-on indica, drawing from East-meets-West indica genetics. It is the progeny of a legendary Los Angeles OG Kush clone and DNA Genetics' LA Confidential strain, bringing a southern Cal indica together with a pure Afghani for a pungent, eye-squinting, high-caliber indica body stone.

As plants, indicas are wonderfully versatile. They're willing to adapt to different growing media, indoor and outdoor environments, and varied growing styles. The Cataract Kush grows robustly in most settings. It is not a racehorse in the vegetation stage, growing at a slower pace than those accustomed to sativas or hybrids will expect. When pinching or super cropping is used, as DNA recommends, these plants will form little bushes. Depending on how vegetative growth is encouraged, plants roughly double in height after forcing flowering. The leaves are a caricature of the indica stereotype: thick, fat leaflets that are dark green to nearly purple in color. As the buds form on this plant, growers will be sure to notice their unique otherworldly silver sheen. They bypass normal green altogether, as if painted from a different palette. Even once the buds are matured, cured, and in the jar, they still radiate a metallic luster.

This plant is not particularly well suited to hotter climates or conditions, which lead to very tight intermodal spacing and disadvantage the yield. Instead this indica prefers temperate weather, favoring the cooler over the hotter, as long as it doesn't freeze or frost. Powdery mildew seems to stay away from the Cataract Kush, and she is not nutrient sensitive. This stuff has a strong, dank, unmistakable smell while growing. The odor only intensifies as this plant flowers. After the proper cure, the smells mature along with the buds for a heady aroma.

Cataract Kush is a connoisseur-grade indica that novices can grow with great results. Even though they can grow this plant easily, they may want to read the warning label first. The Cataract is so named because it brings on the squinty-eyed, Mr. Magoo stone that penetrates deep into the body. This is a heavy stone that creeps up about ten minutes after smoking and keeps building in intensity long after the smoking has ended. Combine that with the creeper effect and it can cause serious couchlock for the uninitiated. Lightweight smokers may have an unpleasant experience if unprepared, but those who are after the big body stone indica will be pleased with the hashy, spicy-sweet flavor that brings the rich pungency of Eastern spices. Medical users will enjoy this strain's usefulness for pain relief, encouragement of appetite, and assistance with sleep.

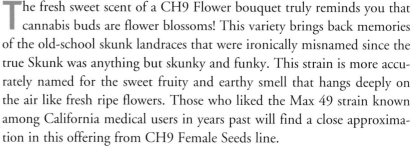

CH9 Flower
CH9 Female Seeds

The fresh sweet scent of a CH9 Flower bouquet truly reminds you that cannabis buds are flower blossoms! This variety brings back memories of the old-school skunk landraces that were ironically misnamed since the true Skunk was anything but skunky and funky. This strain is more accurately named for the sweet fruity and earthy smell that hangs deeply on the air like fresh ripe flowers. Those who liked the Max 49 strain known among California medical users in years past will find a close approximation in this offering from CH9 Female Seeds line.

CH9 Flower is a feminized variety that grows best indoors, but can grow outdoors in hospitable regions where the growing season lasts through the end of October. This plant is versatile and can either be pruned and grown in a sea of green, or allowed to multi-branch in hydro or soil. It branches well and can grow to sizes of 6–7 feet tall (2 meters).

CH9 Flower is a terrific plant for closet cultivating or a home box garden. The buds have enviable crystal production and lush, deep green foliage. The final results possess a delicacy that may impress others who assume such subtlety was challenging in the garden. However, this variety is actually quite agreeable and vigorous, and shows flexibility to mild fluctuations in garden conditions.

Once cured, CH9 Flower has a very uplifting and complex aroma. Because of its lovely and subtle tones of flavor, the CH9 Flower is best appreciated in a vaporizer. Taste connoisseurs will be sure to delight in its naturally aromatic perfume and enjoy it as a flavor experience. The high delivers an energy that is clear and euphoric, cerebral and psychedelic, enticing thought, but also bending the mind in unexpected directions.

 60/40

 energetic, clear, trippy, happy

 fresh, sweet, floral

 65–70 days

 ♀unknown Holland x cubed female pollen of Ed Rosenthal Super Bud, Jack Herer, and Power Plant

 100g per plant in 350g per plant out

 SOG

CH9 G Bolt
CH9 Female Seeds

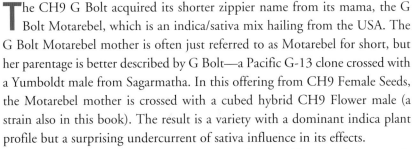

The CH9 G Bolt acquired its shorter zippier name from its mama, the G Bolt Motarebel, which is an indica/sativa mix hailing from the USA. The G Bolt Motarebel mother is often just referred to as Motarebel for short, but her parentage is better described by G Bolt—a Pacific G-13 clone crossed with a Yumboldt male from Sagarmatha. In this offering from CH9 Female Seeds, the Motarebel mother is crossed with a cubed hybrid CH9 Flower male (a strain also in this book). The result is a variety with a dominant indica plant profile but a surprising undercurrent of sativa influence in its effects.

The CH9 G Bolt has dark thick leaves and a vine-like growth pattern. It branches easily and resembles a tropical grape plant. As such, it does better in a screen of green than a sea of green setup. Hydroponics farmers may have an easier time bringing out the strong G Bolt aroma and producing more gland-laden flowers. The G Bolt tends to forgive minor errors and to bounce back when the problem is fixed. This strong vigor makes it a good choice to build beginner confidence.

The CH9 G Bolt was developed mainly for indoor gardens, but grows well outdoors in favorable climates such as America, Australia, and the sunnier parts of Europe. It can handle a broad range of temperatures, including slightly warm or cold temps, without too much complaint. This plant typically matures in 9–10 weeks or can be harvested at the end of October if the crop was planted in mid-April. Average indoor yields are 100 grams per plant. The smell while growing is very fresh, and invigoratingly green. When finished, the buds are frosty and rock hard, and the buzz harkens back to the uplifting and long lasting buzz of its maternal line, the Pacific G-13.

Any grower will have pride in the quality of their CH9 G Bolt harvest. Once cured, this strain retains the woodsy flavor of its Yumboldt grandpappy. The cured buds have a tingly fresh pepper edge with a mild skunky undertone. This variety tends to bring on a euphoric but clear sense of things, making it a functional smoke that can accompany many daytime activities. It also has potential as good medicine, with recommendations for use in anxiety, arthritis, and multiple sclerosis.

I S 70/30

active, clear, happy, long lasting

earthy-fresh and fruity

65 days

G Bolt Motarebel x CH9 Flower

100g per plant in 350g per plant out

SOG

CH9 Jack 33
CH9 Female Seeds

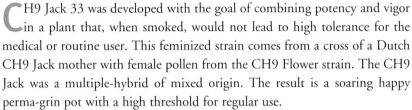

 60/40

 heady, positive, long lasting, clear

 musky

 60–65 days

 ♀CH9 Jack x CH9 Flower feminized pollen

 100g per plant in 300g per plant out

CH9 Jack 33 was developed with the goal of combining potency and vigor in a plant that, when smoked, would not lead to high tolerance for the medical or routine user. This feminized strain comes from a cross of a Dutch CH9 Jack mother with female pollen from the CH9 Flower strain. The CH9 Jack was a multiple-hybrid of mixed origin. The result is a soaring happy perma-grin pot with a high threshold for regular use.

CH9 Jack 33 was intended for indoor gardens, although balmy climates with a long grow season will also allow this strain to move into the great outdoors and still finish by mid-October. This strain is particularly happy when grown with organics. Maximum yields for outdoor plants can be achieved by germinating this plant indoors in February or March and then transplanting outdoors when the weather becomes friendly enough not to jeopardize the plants.

Genetically speaking, these plants slightly favor sativa, but their structure and effects would lead one to overestimate the sativa makeup. The CH9 Jack 33 plant takes on the traditional Christmas tree shape and has thin leaves that fade from dark to light green as the plants ripen. The solid, symmetrical branching and good internodal spacing make this a congenial plant to clone. Clones root well and begin vegetating quickly. On average, these plants reach 6 feet (2 meters) in height at maturity. The buds shine with frost over a medium-dense dark green bud with conspicuous orange hairs. This strain develops a distinctly musky smell as plants reach maturity.

CH9 Jack 33 has a sweet spicy grape aroma with haze undertones, and a clean refreshing feeling in the mouth. The high may bring out your inner hippie or optimistic side, with its expansive and uplifting philosophical effect. It is a strain that can be used to intensify happiness, foster meditation, and inspire creative impulses without sapping the energy needed to act upon them. Given its functional and long lasting effect, it also has potential use as a medicinal for many conditions that don't rely on the heavier indica qualities to provide relief. The CH9 Jack 33 brings easy laughter, and the mild sense of amazement that psychedelics often induce as they take effect.

33

Cheesus
Big Buddha Seeds

When Buddha and Godbud mix it up with the Cheese, it seems only fitting that their progeny would be none other than Cheesus. This strain was developed by young bloods in the Amsterdam breeding scene. The Big Buddha Cheese female is crossed to a male Godbud from British Columbia, courtesy of the BC Bud Depot. In order to feminize the strain, the resulting hybrid was crossed with a reversed Cheesus father to render all seeds feminine.

Cheesus brings indica and sativa together in a hybrid that blends their qualities peacefully. She grows in a slender indica profile and quickly forms a structure that is solid enough to support fat colas. The leaves are a deep healthy green with a chunky indica shape. Cheesus plants do well in a sea of green or in systems that maintain multiple branches. Any growing medium is agreeable, and moderate to heavy feeding is recommended. From the thick green of this plant emerge conical buds that are dense, bringing good yields to those who are attentive, loving, and persistent. Growing Cheesus requires patience, with a lengthy flowering time of 9–12 weeks, but the results may turn you into a believer. Actually, Cheesus serves either the expert or the beginning gardener well, from any creed to none, breeding enjoyment and respect for the plant.

Few growers have the luxury to garden Cheesus outdoors, but those who do can expect to harvest around the end of October. Maximum outdoor sizes average 6–7 feet (2 meters) and deliver per-plant yields of up to 1000 grams for those who wait out the long season.

The Cheesus makes elevating head stash. It is good for everyday use, bringing on a positive and meditative enjoyment. It may encourage a talkative mood, and is not desirable for highly focused work. The flavors are deep and dank: imagine a sweet earthy incense infused with lavender and an edge of tart honey fruitiness and a little pine and spice. Cheesus has many disciples but makes no exclusive claims on your devotions. She doesn't have to—the connoisseur experience speaks for itself.

 60/40

 uplifting, talkative, euphoric

 dank, tart, lavender incense

 65–80 days

 Big Buddha Cheese x ♀BC Godbud X ♂reversed/selfed Cheesus

 200g per plant in 1000g per plant out

 SOG

Chiesel
Big Buddha Seeds

The Chiesel project started in 2006 when friend and master breeder Soma gifted Big Buddha some of his legendary New York City Diesel in seed form. Out of these seeds Big Buddha and his team selected a really nice phenotype of the diesel male to cross with the original Cheese clone.

These seeds were then given to growers in the UK, the Netherlands, and Spain to try out and report on. After the seeds were grown out, the search for a special Chiesel clone began. Big Buddha's breeding mission was to select the one with the most grapefruit-fuel taste. This Chiesel was feminized by reversing it with itself. In November 2008, Chiesel was released.

Chiesel grows like its Cheese mama—a slender but open sativa structure with indica-style leaves. It has hybrid vigor, thriving best when left with many branches and fed generously with nutrients. The buds are like pine cones—compact, oblong, and dense with light electric green coloring and faint orange hairs. Flowering takes about 9 to 10 weeks depending on preferences and conditions. Earlier harvests will yield a taste that leans towards the Cheese/kush profile. When plants are left to flower longer, flavors are a deeper, more grapefruit kush.

Chiesel is smelly and pungent while growing. It brings the old school sublimeness that the Cheese captures together in harmony with the grapefruit fuel kush of the Diesel. The flavors of this weed can serve as a party icebreaker, getting people talking, or circling for a taste of the hashy fuel pungency with a grapefruit sour edge. With Chiesel, the party doesn't end there—this is a very up, energetic pot that has an electric enlivening feel to it. It can lead to giggling and improvisational creativity, and it has enough body balance to bring out a sensual mood when the party is only for two.

 60/40

 uplifting, electric

 fuel, grapefruit, Thai stick

 60–75 days

 UK Cheese x New York City Diesel

 400g per plant in 1200g per plant out

 SOG

Cocoa Kush
DJ Short

Cocoa Kush is a 2009 release from the stables of the Delta-9 collection. It was developed on the US West Coast and tested in Oregon and California. DJ Short's breeding work is most strongly associated with his development of the original Blueberry. A meticulous breeder, DJ has mostly worked to expand the Blue family, creating boutique strains for the medical or hobby grower that are stable, uniquely flavorful first-class headstash.

Cocoa Kush is no exception. Sister to the Vanilluna (also in this book), Cocoa Kush is a selection of two Blueberry parents. Even though they are both Blueberries, they embody different variations: the mother is a more sativa type, and the father is a "stretch" indica type, making Cocoa Kush more similar to an F1 hybrid than an inbred line. The F1 seeds are uniform, but offer genetic diversity in additional crosses. Cocoa Kush's Blueberry sativa mother forms asymmetric growth and often has no dominant main stem. Less than a quarter of the leaves show variegation (the "krinkle" leaf characteristic). By finish, this plant ranges into the deep blue and lavender hues so often associated with the Blueberry strain, and her flavors are tangy, with a subtle chocolate palate.

50/50

soaring, then mellow

tangy, chocolate, licorice

55–65 days

♀Blueberry sativa x ♂Original Blueberry

1g per watt

SOG

The Blue family originated with crosses of four pure P1 landrace varieties: the Highland Thai, Chocolate Thai, Highland Oaxaca Gold, and Afghan indica. The Cocoa Kush is aesthetically and experientially reminiscent of its grandmamma Chocolate Thai. Structurally Cocoa Kush blends kush characteristics and Thai influences. With some help from the indica-leaning Blueberry papa, Cocoa grows as a uniform and symmetric plant with fat dark leaves and compact nodes, but it is not as thickset as an indica, incorporating an open or stretchy aspect in its structure from the sativa lines. Extended vegetative time coupled with early topping is recommended to increase yield, or run these plants un-topped in a sea of green system. After 8–9 weeks of flowering time, these plants reach a medium height with sturdy stems and ample resin that emanates high-end aromatics. Cocoa colas are tight and elongated lavender foxtails. The swollen purpled calyxes are like bunches of grapes along a vine.

Cocoa Kush excels in its complex yet subtle flavors. DJ is a taste master, and with Cocoa Kush, the mixture of flavors includes a zesty fruit edge with a blend of chocolate, tobacco, licorice, and nuts. Remember riding a roller coaster? That moment right after the pause at the top of the first peak, when the wheels start to roll forward into the swift and exhilarating ride ahead? The initial hit of Cocoa Kush has that breathless quality to it. Its intense beginning may make occasional or light users anxious or momentarily overwhelmed. However, not to worry, the sensation tapers into a more mellow, sleepy, and dreamy state of mind.

Crippled Pit
Stoney Girl Gardens

The puzzle of the enigmatically named Crippled Pit, also known as "Crippit," is solved when you realize that it takes one name from each of its parents. "Crippled" comes from the Crippled Rhino mother strain, a cross of the Cannabis Cup winner, White Rhino, and a Crippler Chocolate Thai from Seattle. The "Pit" comes from the "Pit Bull" father strain, a combination of a P-91 female from southern California and Stoney Girl's Sugar Plum strain, the 2003 winner of the Oregon Medical Cannabis Award for Indica.

Bringing these indica-strong winners together in the Crippled Pit has produced a plant that grows like a champ outside as well as indoors. This plant forms a classic umbrella and sports huge leaves and big chunky buds. While indicas are typically short, squat, and bushy plants, the outdoor Crippled Pit plant can easily grow into an 8-foot giant, depending on how the plant is vegetated. Crippit will also gladly grow indoors, giving off a powerful floral smell throughout flowering. Using organics for soil and fertilizer offers great support for maximizing flavor and yields. In climates where the night air turns cools just as fall harvest time approaches, the leaves darken to purple. In more constant climates, the plants will stay green throughout.

Indicas, originally hailing from more temperate regions, are often quicker in their development through the flowering cycle, and Crippit plants are no exception. This variety finishes in about 5 weeks and produces a satisfying yield. When smoked or vaporized, this strain is a strong starter out of the gate and induces a dreamy state of stoniness with a calm, but steady energetic vibration. It has been known to work well for nausea and offers some strong medicinal qualities. Those who try Crippled Pit notice its highly desirable balance of flavors. It hits a Thai top note and a Hawaiian base flavor, with an earthy sweet tone that never gets too saccharine. The big leaves churn out some nice bubble hash, too.

I

calm, cheerful, stoney, electric

hashy chocolate, earthy tropical

35–42 days

♀Crippled Rhino x ♂Pit Bull

200g per plant in 1500g per plant out

Stoney Girl Gardens

Stoney Girl Gardens was founded in Oregon in 1999 by Jennifer Valley a fourth-stage cancer patient who is an avid activist and medical cardholder. Valley began her first grow, a modest closet garden, with no horticulture experience, relying on a sea of half-baked grow information. Her first harvest was so unfortunate it left her in tears. She realized she needed hands-on assistance, and with the help of an experienced grower, she was able to learn some easy strategies to reach garden success.

Marijuana has allowed Valley to reduce healthcare costs, eliminate many prescription medications while improving health indicators, and even to thrive in many ways. Encouraged by her improvement and determined to aid her fellow medical patients, Valley not only got her garden growing, but helped grow a philanthropic minded group of masterful breeders and horticulturists with decades of experience and a wealth of knowledge. This led to the formation of Stoney Girl Gardens, a private group of patients and caregivers inspired by patients and dedicated to bringing good genetics and growing techniques to the medical marijuana community. She says, "Most of the patients I have worked with, including myself, are living much longer than their doctors ever expected."

As a 30-year cancer patient, Valley's mission is to help make the best medicine possible for other patients who are facing severe pain or are facing terminal conditions. Stoney Girl Gardens has tested over 100 species, always holding in mind the limitations within which medical users in the US must grow, and always selecting strains that best fit these criteria.

So far, Stoney Girl Gardens has taken first-prize awards twice: once in November 2002 and again in November 2003. The Stoney Girl signature series includes true breeding strains such as Pit Bull, Crippled Rhino, Berkeley Blues, Oregon Pinot Noir, and Sugar Plum. These Pacific Northwest strains are currently only available to qualified medical marijuana candidates in the US.

Critical #47
Positronics Seeds SL

The Critical #47 is a 50/50 hybrid whose name is also half-and-half, taking "Critical" from the mother breed and "#47" from the AK father. The mother Critical strain is an Afghani Skunk cross. The father is an AK-47 with genetics from Mexico, Colombia, and India. Critical #47 develops quickly and realizes its complete genetic potential when grown in soil outdoors. Critical Mass and AK-47 improve on Skunk varieties and in their cross, the skunky flavor increases.

This variety grows vigorously and branches prodigiously, forming many extremely serrated leaves. Critical #47 reaches a medium-tall height. Two weeks of vegetative time is sufficient to allow plants to take root, and vegetating much longer may result in oversized stalks. For those interested in clones, Critical #47 is ideal because a great number of cuttings can be taken from its branchy structure.

Positronics recommends pruning after the third week of flowering to better direct the enormous potential that this plant shows. The green flowers give off a strong smell between mango and peach, with hints of vanilla. Organic fertilizers allow this plant to form healthy and flavorful buds. Critical #47 finishes flowering after 7 weeks. Outdoors, these plants show signs of maturity during August and can typically be harvested by the end of September.

Critical #47 plants should be supported since the weight of the floral bunches will overpower the slender stalks During growth, this variety does not require large amounts of fertilizer, but turns yellow quickly if it is suffering from an NPK nutritional deficiency, making basic nutrient needs easy to detect. When grown near curious neighbors or in stealth indoor systems, an odor control system such as carbon filtering is a necessity—without some precautions, Critical #47 emits telltale olfactory evidence of its presence.

At maturity, this plant reaches an average height of 5 feet (1.5 meters) and delivers yields that range from $1/2$ to 1 pound (250–500g) per plant. The Critical #47 buzz is calm with lucid sativa influences and a touch of the munchies. In terms of taste, this variety is a skillful blend of two sweet varieties that deliver a fruity mango-peach flavor infused with vanilla overtones.

 50/50

 calm, lucid, munchies

 mango, peach, vanilla

 50–55 days

 ♀Critical/Afghani Skunk x ♂AK-47

 400g per m² in 500g per plant out

Crystalberry
Seeds of Freedom

Crystalberry is the star child of a breeding program that selected from crosses using two popular and well loved varieties: the Sensi Star and DJ Short's Blueberry. Both of Crystalberry's indica-dominant parents have the distinction of ranging outside the expected indica-driven high. Crystalberry brings together the potent indica body stone with a hint of surprisingly heady euphoria usually reserved for more sativa-leaning strains. This variety allows the parental qualities to shine through in its impressively prismatic sheen of resin, producing a more cerebral indica that hash fans will favor.

Thick and sturdy in stature, Crystalberry looks like an indica and grows to a respectable yet compact size. When forced to flower at 12–16 inches, this strain reaches a height of roughly 3 feet (1 meter) at maturity, so even smaller garden spaces can manage multi-branch plants. Multi-branching is a good strategy since Crystalberry is moderately branchy by nature, especially at the bottom of the plant; however, this plant also adapts readily to a sea of green garden with diligent pruning. Crystalberry plants are vigorous and do not share the trait of initial slow growth with their Blueberry father. Beginners can grow this plant with good success.

Outdoors, these plants become broad bushes that will reach 6–8 feet in height. The Crystalberry smell is not too strong when grown undisturbed, but on closer inspection, the buds reveal their wonderful candy-berry hash fragrance. Compared with other varieties, Crystalberry yields are moderate. Outdoors, yields of 10-plus ounces (300g) can be reached when the plants are allowed to establish themselves and grow to full size. Crystalberry buds are dense and dank, producing color hues of purple and blue from the Blueberry genetics. Where this plant may outshine others is in gland production, which follows in papa Sensi Star's footsteps. Call them crystals, call them berries, either way, the glands are large enough that they can be seen easily without magnification. For those who like to recycle their foliage, Crystalberry will impress with a generous quantity of tasty and potent bubble hash.

The smoke is blueberry tasting with Star's pungent lemon overtones. Medical users who rely on the indica to help with pain management but prefer a more head-focused high may find these qualities all wrapped up in the Crystalberry bud.

 I S 80/20

 intense, long lasting, narcotic

 berry-haze candy

 49–56 days

 ♀SensiStar F2 x ♂DJ Short Blueberry

 50g per plant in 300g per plant out

 SOG

Dancehall
Reggae Seeds

Photos: Lajuanna

In Jamaican popular music, Dancehall style tunes are the music of celebration. This upbeat variant from Reggae Seeds is a perfect complement to its musical namesake, with a lively and lighthearted social effect that enhances life's rhythms.

Dancehall's mother is a hybrid of Mexican, Afghan, and Spanish origins called Juanita La Lagrimosa. The Father is a strain named Kalijah, a combination of Blue Heaven and Mexican-Afghani genetics. Together in the Dancehall strain, these genetics result in a hardy plant with uniquely nuanced flavors that are enhanced by using organic methods in soil.

Dancehall's pace of growth begins moderately, but it picks up a faster beat once flower forcing is initiated. It is better to keep the vegetative time short to avoid space issues later, especially if the garden is in a sea of green style. The Dancehall plant only branches minimally, but likes to grow longer branches low on the plant. Indoors, it takes 8 to 9 weeks to finish.

Outdoors, Dancehall is well adapted to Spain's climate and will thrive in dry regions. When planted in April or May, this plant finishes in about 150 days and is ready to harvest in September or October, depending on conditions. The final height can range from 5–8 feet (1.5–2.5 meters). Proper care will lead to satisfying outdoor yields ranging from 400g to a kilogram (roughly 1–2 pounds) per plant. Water is key for this variety. Dancehall needs low humidity and moist soil at all times to thrive. In areas with higher humidity, the compact, elongated buds are susceptible to botrytis (gray fungus). While this plant is sensitive about watering, it is not an otherwise delicate plant and will grow in cold or hot conditions.

As Dancehall reaches maturity, the leaves and buds add reds, blues, and purples to the green, and all is kissed with white sticky resin. Growers who like the vibrant tones of chromatic buds will enjoy Dancehall's final appearance. Buds may show reflowering toward the end.

Dancehall is a pleasure for all the senses. While not particularly aromatic during growth, once its long, compact buds are cracked open, the complex odors of forest and spicy incense mix with a touch of acidic fruit and haze to tantalize the palate. The flavor mixes fruits with a green mossy flavor and a touch of haze, and lingers on the tongue in a satisfying way. Dancehall is a party weed that pairs well with a long night of dancing to Jamaican grooves. It has a progressive enduring effect that inspires an alert, creative, and sociable mood. In its first appearance at a cannabis cup event, Dancehall won first place in the 2010 Spannabis indoor bio category.

 60/40

 cerebral, creative, lively

 forest, incense

 55–65 days

 ♀Juanita La Lagrimosa x ♂Kalijah

 350–500g per m²

SOG

REGGAE SEEDS

At Reggae Seeds, plants are conferred a reggae style based upon their rhythm, freshness, and creativity. We are dedicated to finding and breeding little treasures to contribute to the diversity of high quality cannabis. It is our mission to focus on regular seeds in the Reggae family, because we believe that males are very important and that the knowledge of differentiating male and female plants and selecting genetic crosses from mothers and fathers offers an important wealth to the cannabis world. Our Reggae family line began in 2006 and continues to develop with plants that are acclimated for outdoor grows but whose low, minimal-branching structures make them suitable to indoor spaces as well.

Here at Reggae Seeds, we like to eat naturally and organically, and to stay chemical free and without genetic manipulation of our foods. We apply the same philosophy to cannabis gardening and breeding. We believe this is better for the sake of our health and for the conservation of biodiversity.

We encourage hobby breeders to find the joy that comes with making their own mixes and strains, to taste, discover, create, and plant—and in sum, to enjoy this precious plant.

Dark Star
TH Seeds

I

narcotic, stupefying

mellow, nutty

65–70 days

♀Purple Kush x ♂Mazar-I-Sharif

400–500g per m²

Strictly speaking, a "dark star" is the term for a celestial object that, due to its immense mass, traps light in its overwhelming gravity, rendering it dark. This is an antiquated term and is now more commonly known as a black hole. But chances are good that the name "Dark Star" did not lead you to think about astronomy. Chances are, if you ever listened to the Grateful Dead, right now you are thinking of the epic song that served as the bedrock upon which hours of improvisational music were built. The song became so associated with the Dead that it was adopted by the Dark Star Orchestra, a unique tribute band who has been meticulously recreating specific Dead shows from the vast catalog of their 30-year tour history. With this strain, you may also be recreating a little something special of your own from the touring days.

The Dark Star strain is quintessential old-school stoner weed. An all-indica cross, Dark Star matches the timeless Purple Kush with a true landrace indica from the Khyber Pass in Afghanistan, the domain from which indicas first evolved. This is the weed you hoped you were getting from the skunky smelling hippie on the way into the show. It is a quick onset, long lasting indica buzz ideal for spacing out and letting the music take over.

The Dark Star plant is classic Afghan in structure, growing thick, strong branches at a slow pace, which requires a little patience in vegetative phase and may cause some early anxiety for beginners who expect a more typical indica timetable. This plant is slower than many of its brethren and works best as an indoor plant, where it will take 9–10 weeks to reach full ripened bloom. Once flowering, this plant forms a large main cola that is encircled by a crown of budlets. Dark Star flowers, like their cosmic namesake, are super dense and compact. The leaves are wide and so dark that the deep greens take on a blue tinge. When ready to harvest, Dark Star's color changes quickly, with the spiky bud hairs turning pink-red. This plant's clones set slowly, but mature plants are easy to manicure.

The Dark Star high is stupefying and narcotic, with spacey, otherworldly qualities. While its aroma is not overpowering, it is interesting with mellow, almost nutty, flavors. The onset is fast, and the high will last through a concert or make for a great afternoon. This is not a functional buzz for accomplishing tasks, especially if they involve reading or counting. Dark Star will likely add another dimension to aesthetic or sensory experiences, and acts as an appetite enhancer or pain reliever for medicinal users.

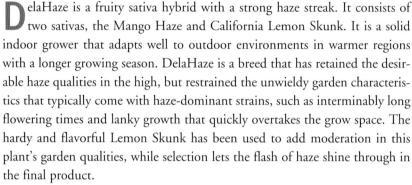

DelaHaze
Paradise Seeds

DelaHaze is a fruity sativa hybrid with a strong haze streak. It consists of two sativas, the Mango Haze and California Lemon Skunk. It is a solid indoor grower that adapts well to outdoor environments in warmer regions with a longer growing season. DelaHaze is a breed that has retained the desirable haze qualities in the high, but restrained the unwieldy garden characteristics that typically come with haze-dominant strains, such as interminably long flowering times and lanky growth that quickly overtakes the grow space. The hardy and flavorful Lemon Skunk has been used to add moderation in this plant's garden qualities, while selection lets the flash of haze shine through in the final product.

Even though the dominant sativa-haze composition has been tempered in this cross, DelaHaze still has a tendency to stretch if vegetated for too long. Paradise recommends inducing flowering early, before the plants gain too much height. A 9-week flowering time is short for a haze-influenced strain. To appreciate her fully let her flower one week extra. The fine citrus/haze flowers will fill the growroom with a beautiful aroma containing hints of citrus and mango in the dominant haze scent.

DelaHaze has potent THC levels yet still delivers ample yields. Indoor per-plant yields on multi-branch plants can reach 2 ounces (50g). Plants are best with multiple branches, and when vegetative time is managed properly, the increase in size during flowering will remain within a manageable range, around 3 feet (1 meter).

Haze fans have given this strain connoisseur ratings and reviews. The flavor is haze with sweet fruity accents. The high is a creeper with a clear-headed transition. DelaHaze is an active functional mood lifting buzz that avoids both heavy and sedating physical effects and the speedy or trippy mental quickening that some head highs induce. Instead, the sensation has a calm clarity, smoothing out the doldrums, and lightening the spirit to engage a more positive state of mind. A mild and pleasant body relaxation effect is often felt after some time has passed.

DelaHaze was winner of 2nd prize in the Cannabis Champions Cup in Spain in 2009.

 70/30

 clear, active, soaring

 mango-citrus haze

 63–70 days

 Mango Haze x California Lemon Skunk

 500g per m² in 1 kg per plant out

 in preferred

Diabolic Funxta
Don't Panic Organix

Diabolic Funxta is a blissful mix of American-bred varieties. The mother is an East Coast Sour Diesel and the father is an American Funxta, a triple inbred cross (IBX) of the Platinum OG Kush inbred line (IBL). While the Kush parent is known for high quality, dreamy buds, it tends to be tall, lanky, and low yielding. The Sour Diesel mama is a bulkier gal with more generous yields. Some people really like the strong flavors of the Sour Diesel as well as its jet-fueled stoney qualities that quickly reach high altitudes.

Diabolic Funxta's sativa-dominant parentage inclines her to grow taller than average plants, with average indoor heights easily topping 5 feet but usually staying under 6 feet. At the outset, these big "Cali Kush"-style plants resemble smaller sisters to a true Haze, but as they progress, they gain a thicker density, losing the wispiness typical of haze plants. Diabolic Funxta is better as a multi-branch plant, rather than trying to tame her to a sea of green, although if you must use a sea of green technique, force flowering early on. When allowed to branch, DF plants resemble large Jewish menorahs. Indoor plants finish about 2 weeks quicker when grown hydro instead of soil.

When grown outdoors from seed, Diabolic Funxta takes a total of 5–6 months. Outdoor plants become massive, easily growing to heights between 9 and 11 feet. In California, DF's growth cycle typically translates to a late October or early November harvest. This variety thrives in areas throughout the southwestern US where seeds have been tested in multiple locations and found to perform well in both humid and dry regions. Diabolic Funxta likes good rich soil and light nutrients.

DF plants form 5 to 6 long thick diamond-shaped main colas, or even more when they are topped or super-cropped. As the buds become fuller, they swell in a corkscrew shape and begin to acquire the strong diesel-kush aroma. Average indoor yields improve upon the father Kush, producing 4–5 ounces (115g) per plant. Outside, 3–4 pounds per plant is a reasonable expectation. This variety is flexible, showing little to no stress during transplanting and cloning.

The Diabolic Funxta is perhaps more funky than diabolical. Its high is cheerful with effects that reverberate through the mind and body like a wild drum solo. The flavor blends the diesel kush parentage, combining a strong sour diesel citrus aroma with a smooth floral kush taste, and a heavy diesel exhale that lingers on the tongue. Medicinally, it has worked well for eye pressure, lower back pain, migraines, multiple sclerosis, and wasting syndrome.

S I 70/30

clear, inspirational

citrus diesel

60–70 days

♀ East Coast Sour Diesel x ♂ Funxta's Triple Kush

100g per plant in 1000g per plant out

Oakland: Cannabis Liberated Zone
by Bill Weinberg

As the Bay Area's second city, Oakland tends to be overlooked by tourists and media in favor of its more fabled and sexy sibling across the water, San Francisco. Yet in the cannabis revolution that is blossoming across the Golden State, Oakland is more advanced in manifesting the Californian ethic of living in the future. Where cannabis is concerned, Oakland is in the vanguard of all California's municipalities in building a working model of what an herb-friendly culture and economy could look like.

Radical Roots

Oakland has always been more of a working-class town than San Francisco. In the 1960s Oakland was the crucible of the Black Panthers, who armed in defense against police brutality and launched self-help initiatives like free children's breakfast programs. Simultaneously, at the other end of Telegraph Avenue on the UC Berkeley campus, anti-war protests followed the Free Speech Movement spearheading the radicalization of the East Bay. Protests at the Oakland Induction Center, where local youth were readied for deployment to Vietnam, were a key point of cross-fertilization between the Berkeley student radicals and Oakland community activists.

Cultural refugees from Middle America were of course pouring into the Bay Area in those years, psychedelicizing the whole megalopolis and turning it into a laboratory for social change and cultural experimentation. But while the mass media focused on San Francisco's "Summer of Love" in 1967, a more politically sharp counter-culture was blooming on the eastern side of the iconic Bay Bridge.

In the 1970s, as Oakland suffered from urban blight, hippies from the Bay Area began colonizing California's North Coast. Humboldt County especially became a world-class center of cannabis cultivation. The initial seed stock was sativa saved from the Mexican imports they'd been smoking; later, some local growers journeyed to Afghanistan to bring back indica seeds, creating the distinctive sativa-indica hybrid known as "Skunk #1," which actually has a sweet rather than acrid smell. Harvest time saw much of the crop going down Highway 101 to the urban market in the Bay Area. Eventually indoor cultivation began within the Bay Area itself. The cannabis economy was now well established, if underground.

Oakland activists including, from the left, Ed Rosenthal, Richard Lee, Rebecca Kaplan, campaign worker, and Dale Clare.

Berkeley rents soared in the 1980s, leading more hippies to move to North Oakland. In a predictable pattern of urban development, North Oakland started gentrifying in the 1990s; real estate interests re-christened the district "Temescal." Today, anarchists, punks, and earthies still live in collective houses scattered around the area. Oakland's down-at-the-heels popular image has held back its bourgeois fashionability—leaving more space for authentic culture.

The hippies and alternative types are just one part of Oakland's multicultural mix. Oakland's Chinatown, while lacking a characteristic entry arch, is more pan-Asian and far less touristy than San Francisco's Chinatown. Even East Oakland, with its reputation for crime and danger, has a vibrant hip-hop scene pioneered by artists like Too $hort. In recent years, urban back-to-the-land'ers have started moving in, turning their backyards into functioning farms and striving towards self-sufficiency amidst the blight.

If Oakland's alternative scene was launched by rent refugees from Berkeley and San Francisco, it soon took on a life if its own, with more cultural radicals and visionaries attracted by the growing community. It was only a matter of time before this community began to flex its political muscle. An early harbinger came with the 1995 city council vote to de-fund the DARE program, following a long grassroots activist campaign. The council's Public Safety Committee agreed in a meeting with the police department to eliminate the heavy-handed anti-drug propaganda program.

The passage of Proposition 215, the historic 1996 California state initiative that instated the country's first medical marijuana law, was a victory that energized the scene with a new sense of possibilities and awareness. The process of transformation that began in the sixties was maturing, normalizing, and ready to come into its own.

And now in the area around the three-way intersection of Telegraph, Broadway and 15th Street, just above the heart of downtown Oakland, the USA's foremost enclave of liberated cannabis culture has emerged. Dubbed "Oaksterdam" by local activists and entrepreneurs—an obvious play on Amsterdam—the official slogan for this neighborhood is "Dutch freedom without the jetlag!"

The Road to Oaksterdam

San Francisco may have led the way in establishing high-profile cannabis clubs after California voters approved Prop 215. But now it is Oakland that is leading the way towards the normalization of our favorite herb.

The Oakland Cannabis Buyers' Cooperative was established immediately upon passage of 215. When the federal government ordered it closed, the Oakland coop took its case all the way to the Supreme Court. But alas, in the 2001 *US vs. OCBC* the high court rejected the medical necessity defense and upheld the power of the federal government to enforce its cannabis laws even in states with medical marijuana legislation on the books.

During this time the internationally known "Guru of Ganja" Ed Rosenthal was deputized as an officer of the City of Oakland to produce cannabis for medical use, leading to another important legal battle. In February 2002 Rosenthal was arrested by federal agents for growing some 100 plants in an Oakland warehouse. Barred in the courtroom from even mentioning his official relationship with Oakland's municipal authorities, he was convicted on three counts of cultivation and conspiracy. But in a humiliating setback for the feds, he was sentenced by District Court Judge Charles Breyer in June 2003 to one symbolic day in prison and a $1,000 fine. He had faced a maximum of 100 years and fines up to $4.5 million.

Rosenthal nonetheless challenged his conviction before the Ninth Circuit Court of Appeals in San Francisco and won. Then in an obvious case of vindictive prosecution, the US Attorney for California's Northern District brought new charges, and Rosenthal

The famous Bulldog Cafe

was re-convicted. But it was the proverbial Pyrrhic victory for the feds; back in Breyer's courtroom, he received credit for time served (his one day behind bars after the first conviction). Although officially a convicted felon, Rosenthal was a free man.

Undaunted by federal intransigence, in November 2004 Oakland voters approved Measure Z making private sales, cultivation, and possession of cannabis the city's lowest police priority. The measure, which won by 65%, also calls on the city to tax and regulate cannabis as soon as possible under California law. It also established a Community Oversight Committee to assure that the new policy is enforced. This was the turning point that led to the emergence of Oaksterdam.

Anatomy of the Liberated Zone

Although Measure Z does not apply to public cannabis use, street dealing, sale to minors or motor vehicle violations, it has allowed the establishment of the United States' first Dutch-style (or *almost* Dutch-style) cannabis coffee houses. The premier such establishment is the Bulldog Coffee Shop at 1739 Broadway. While it certainly exercises far more discretion than Amsterdam coffeeshops, the Bulldog is considered Oakland's first "Measure Z coffeeshop."

Nearby is the Blue Sky Coffee Shop at 377 17th Street, which is actually licensed by the city of Oakland as a medical marijuana dispensary. The Blue Sky was originally called SR-71 after the sleek high-altitude military aircraft, until defense giant Lockheed-Martin threatened to sue.

In a compromise with city authorities, on-site consumption is not permitted at licensed dispensaries like Blue Sky, but all sorts of goodies are available, from cannabis-laced cheesecake, peanut brittle, and salad

Oaksterdam's Vince Wallace and Jennifer Clevinger's ...intet

dressing, to good old straight-up bud. Many of these products are from the local outfit Compassion Medicinal Edibles (formerly known as Tainted Inc.) whose founder Mickey Martin was busted by the feds for his efforts in 2007. Martin pleaded guilty to "conspiracy to manufacture a mixture or substance containing marijuana" although he avoided prison time in the end.

Meanwhile, the OCBC continued to function as a clearinghouse for Oakland's medicinal users even after it ceased to be an actual dispensary following its legal defeat. In 2008 it was re-christened the Patient ID Center or PIDC, now located at 1733 Broadway, another hub of Oaksterdam. Unlike the old OCBC, the PIDC doesn't distribute cannabis, but establishes who under state law is entitled to purchase cannabis at licensed dispensaries or to grow their own. It issues tamper-proof ID cards and maintains a 24-hour hotline that can be used by patients and law enforcement alike. Off-site doctors decide who's accepted as a legitimate user under 215, and the PIDC verifies and maintains the records.

The PIDC-issued card is also known as the "city card" since the center is licensed by the city. The PIDC likewise accepts the "state card" issued by Alameda County Patient Services under the statewide Medical Marijuana Identification Card Program (MMICP). The MMICP came into being after the passage in Sacramento of the wryly named State Bill 420. Under the 2003 law, patients can use the ID card as evidence that they have received a recommendation from their physician to use medicinal cannabis.

While not open to the public and maintained at a secret location, Oaksterdam Nursery is what makes much of the scene happen. Under grow lights, a sea of fragrant plants ascend from big pots filled with rock wool, coco fiber, and special nutrients providing strong medicine to the enclave's public establishments. Typical strains developed by Oaksterdam Nursery include the sativa-dominant Shiva Skunk, indica-heavy Purple Kush, and hybridized Deep Chunk X Strawberry Cough. From here, starter plants are provided for patients and dispensaries around Oakland and its environs.

And finally, the brightest star in the Oaksterdam constellation is Oaksterdam University. Each semester at 1600 Broadway, a new crop of students learns the techniques of marijuana cultivation, through both

Oaksterdam is helping to revive downtown Oakland.

Inside Oaksterdam University

hands-on experience and the study of Oaksterdam-produced instructional materials with names like "Cannabis Yields and Dosage." The university conducts weekend seminars, semester courses, and special lectures. As of 2010, more than 11,000 students have been provided skills useful to the burgeoning cannabis industry.

In May 2010 Oaksterdam University took a big step towards mainstream legitimacy and resolved an outstanding internal dispute with the announcement that the school is unionizing. Some 100 employees at Oaksterdam and five related enterprises (dispensaries, nurseries) voted to join the Bay Area's UFCW Local 5. Separate elections were also verified at hydroponics equipment retailer iGrow in south Oakland and cultivation company AgraMed in the waterfront Embarcadero district. Oakland councilmember and mayoral candidate Rebecca Kaplan joined Oaksterdam employees at a press conference to announce a new coalition for local cannabis workers' rights.

And the cannabis college idea is catching on: the University of Cannabis recently opened in south Oakland, near the airport. Numerous other such institutions are planned around the Bay Area and around the state.

Model for the Future?

Oaksterdam University founder Richard Lee also emerged as the key bankroller and political mastermind of the Tax Cannabis 2010 statewide voter initiative aimed at effectively legalizing marijuana in California. When the campaign was launched, the University's former digs at 1776 Broadway became its headquarters. After the campaign, Lee hopes to turn the location into the Oaksterdam Museum.

Lee says he envisions Oakland becoming home to "hundreds of cannabis coffeeshops, bringing in tourists and creating jobs and generating tax revenue for the city." And he really thinks it is possible. "Lots of activists have settled here and worked hard to make this

Richard Lee, Oaksterdam founder, doing media interview.

happen. Oakland is a very progressive place."

"Oakland is the epicenter of the political change for cannabis," adds Ed Rosenthal. "We are moving from a policy of contention to a policy of cooperation."

Indeed, Measure F, approved by the city's voters in July 2009, imposed a local sales tax on cannabis sold at licensed dispensaries. Legislation is currently pending before Oakland's city council that would permit, tax, and regulate large indoor grow operations like AgraMed. As with the statewide Tax Cannabis initiative, proponents are plugging it as a key solution to chronic budgetary shortfalls.

Oakland's cannabis proponents also joined with other progressive activists to support the mayoral candidacy of Rebecca Kaplan in the November 2010 elections. Kaplan was a key supporter of Measure F and sees the cannabis economy as a part of what her campaign calls the "Oakland renaissance."

The October 2006 opening of Harborside Health Center, Oakland's largest and finest state-of-the-art dispensary, was a key step towards this renaissance. At 1840 Embarcadero, the HHC is the brainchild of Stephen D'Angelo, who came to California to pursue his dream in 1998 after Congress refused to implement a voter-approved medical marijuana law in his home Washington, DC. Viewing cannabis in the context of a greater commitment to holistic medical treatment, the Center offers free acupuncture, chiropractic care, naturopathy, and yoga and Reiki sessions as well as the finest in locally produced cannabis.

Meanwhile, the last entry on the list of the liberated enclave's cannabis-themed institutions is the

Harborside samples on display; note the THC designation

Oaksterdam Gift Shop at 405 15th Street with an on-site Oaksterdam Bike Rental.

Oaksterdam is a major part of the general revitalization of the once-blighted downtown area, best symbolized by the 2008 re-opening of the historic and resplendent Fox Theater on the 80th anniversary of its original grand opening. The landmark theater at 1807 Telegraph is the hub of what city planners are now calling "Uptown" (because it is immediately north of Downtown). While Uptown follows Telegraph Avenue, the parallel Oaksterdam follows Broadway with the two revitalized enclaves coming together where the arteries meet at 15th Street.

Visit Oaksterdam now and witness a working model for the future in a saner and mellower America.

Dr. Grinspoon
Barney's Farm

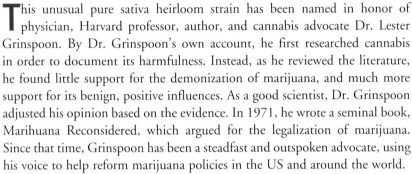

This unusual pure sativa heirloom strain has been named in honor of physician, Harvard professor, author, and cannabis advocate Dr. Lester Grinspoon. By Dr. Grinspoon's own account, he first researched cannabis in order to document its harmfulness. Instead, as he reviewed the literature, he found little support for the demonization of marijuana, and much more support for its benign, positive influences. As a good scientist, Dr. Grinspoon adjusted his opinion based on the evidence. In 1971, he wrote a seminal book, Marihuana Reconsidered, which argued for the legalization of marijuana. Since that time, Grinspoon has been a steadfast and outspoken advocate, using his voice to help reform marijuana policies in the US and around the world.

The aptly named Dr. Grinspoon variety is a "thinking man's" sativa of the highest order. This top-shelf connoisseur breed is a good addition to personal gardens seeking premium headstash. The plant has a distinct flowering pattern that makes it a standout in the garden. The pure sativa heritage means Dr. Grinspoon forms long twig-like branches with the buds loosely strung popcorn-style along the willowy stems. As the plants mature, they begin to fill gaps between bud sites, but the buds remain distinct rather than gathering into one large flower. Yields are moderate with harvests up to 350 grams per square meter. Yields are likely to be better under the tutelage of a gardener who has already grown a few crops and figured out the basics.

The long season makes this an indoor or greenhouse variety when living outside of the equatorial region. Outdoors, Dr. Grinspoon needs 6 full months of agreeable weather to finish, ripening in late October or early November. Using organic fertilizers in soil will bring out the best flavors. The Dr. Grinspoon variety tends to interest gardeners with some experience and a desire for great sativa qualities. It is not "fast-food" style weed for those wanting a quick crop. This is more like a bottle of good champagne. Although Dr. Grinspoon has an effervescent lucidity that makes it suitable for any occasion, these buds are often treasured and reserved to celebrate special moments.

The aroma has the tropical-floral elements expected of an island sativa, but there is also a distinct lemon-herbal sumac smell. These notes are carried through in the flavor, imparting a light lemon tang and a touch of honeyed earthiness. This strain's clarity will be manna for the true aficionado. Dr. Grinspoon has a pleasant entry into the high, inviting a blissful and expansive mood that enhances compassion and provokes intellectual insights. It is very compatible as a daytime smoke or for long evenings with friends, intimate conversations, and deep enjoyment. Given the heightened awareness it encourages, it is less suitable right before retiring for sleep. The effects of Dr. Grinspoon taper off gradually, leaving one as clearheaded at finish as they were at the outset, only quite possibly with a host of new ideas and pleasant experiences to remember.

S

electric, euphoric

honey, earthy

100 days

♀sativa x
♂sativa

50g per plant in
200g per plant out

in preferred

Dr. Grinspoon – A Champion for Legalization

"One day, I hope, we will look back and wonder why our societies were so perverse as to treat cannabis as they did for the greater part of the twentieth century."
—Dr. Lester Grinspoon

Dr. Grinspoon's first foray into the world of cannabis began with a research project nearly 40 years ago. At the time, Lester Grinspoon was an associate professor of psychiatry at Harvard Medical School. It was the end of the 1960s, and the exponential rise of marijuana use among American youth concerned him. He was sure that young people, oblivious to the dangers, were smoking cannabis to their own detriment, and given his background as a medical doctor and academic researcher, he approached it in the way one might expect—by studying the problem. However, the more he reviewed the scientific and medical literature, the less he found to support his position. As a reputable scientist, Dr. Grinspoon kept an open mind and, rather than clinging rigidly to his initial view, he was compelled by the evidence to reverse his opinion and acknowledge marijuana's beneficence. This change of position from marijuana as menace to marijuana as harmless was the basis for his 1971 book *Marihuana Reconsidered.*

Back in the 1970s, Dr. Grinspoon had optimistically believed that the laws would change within the decade. It seemed obvious that the evidence and the laws were in contradiction. The only rational thing to do would be to change the law to reflect the reality. As we all know, when it comes to marijuana, rational policy has been a rare commodity.

Of course, since the 1970s, much new research bolsters Dr. Grinspoon's position. Since that time, Dr. Grinspoon has continued to use his considerable skills to advocate for legalization, publicly speaking and writing on the merits of cannabis, and serving as a public voice to help counteract the damaging misinformation on this plant. He has served as an expert witness in dozens of trials, and testified before Congress. He continues to insist that marijuana's most dangerous aspect is its criminalized status. Dr. Grinspoon's impeccable credentials and impressive position at Harvard have lent great credibility to claims of marijuana's safety. It took much bravery and integrity to go against society's views.

Finally, in the last decade, the work and bravery of many activists has started a wave of change in the law, although there is still more to be done. Correcting the misinformation about marijuana has required prolonged effort, and we are thankful to Dr. Grinspoon for bringing his intelligence, eloquence, and good humor to righting this wrong. It is the work of pioneers such as Lester Grinspoon that has led the way to greater sanity in our treatment of this amazingly diverse plant.

Dready Kush
Humboldt Seed Organisation

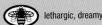

lethargic, dreamy

sweet, pungent

4–5 oz. per plant

63–70 days

♀ original Hindu Kush x ♂ Hindu Kush

in preferred

SOG

Dready Kush is an all-indica strain with strong roots in cannabis meccas both east and west. The genetics come from the Hindu Kush region, the traditional center of cannabis culture and home to the archetypal cannabis indica. Located in the UK, the Humboldt Seed Organisation has been gathering seed stock to create a library of high quality connoisseur cannabis. This includes the strains used in the Dready Kush cross, which have never been commercially available before. This company utilizes the work of many master European breeders. Dready Kush is the work of Humboldt's accomplished in-house breeder, Dready Bob, best known for his work in *Weed World* magazine.

Dready Kush is a short squat plant with dark waxy green leaves that are jagged and thick. Although it can be bushy as are many indicas, the side branching is not significant, and it prefers to form a main stem. Sea of green systems work well. This plant does best with a medium to high EC, between 1.6 and 2.0. When forced at 12 inches (30 cm), the plants are about 16 inches (40cm) at finish and yield 4–5 ounces per plant on average. To reach maximum potential, run-to-waste systems suit this strain best.

Dready Kush flowers do not make many pistils, but the calyxes become very big near the end of flowering. This strain has strong resistance to bud rot and holds up well in a wide range of situations, although it obviously likes its comfort zone. At finish, this plant is picture-perfect, healthy, and vigorous with well-shaped, compact, and pungent buds. The strong smell translates to an amazing sweet earthy hash-haze flavor.

The Dready Kush buzz is definitely a downer, and takes hold fast. A few hits wipe the short-term memory, making it a good interruption for an unproductive train of thought, but less than ideal for tasks such as reading that require a level of focus to be maintained. When used by the uninitiated or smoked in big doses, this strain can induce paranoia or cause a zone out on the couch. This stone can be dreamy or mind numbing; either way, it tends to create some serious downtime in your day or evening, and encourages sleep. Oils made from Dready Kush are very good for medical applications that call for super-duty indica effects.

Dutch Haze
Dutch Passion

Haze strains have a loyal fan base, and with good reason. Hazes are known for their smooth transition into a soaring lucid, cerebral, and extraordinarily euphoric high. The main downside with Haze is horticultural. Fast-starting, tall and willowy plants, Hazes are known to have long flowering times, taking as long as 3 or 4 months in the flowering phase before ripening. In addition, the bolting size of the Haze has to be carefully managed as does its finicky response to conditions. Even when conditions are managed perfectly, these plants still often deliver lower than average yields. When breeders try to improve the gardening characteristics, it often comes at the expense of losing some of the haze effect in the high.

Dutch Passion's answer for the haze enthusiast is the Dutch Haze strain. This mostly sativa, all-haze variety was developed from Dutch Passion's extensive genetic seed bank and network of breeding expertise. Breeders grew out hundreds of plants, crossing top North American and European haze strains, and then subjecting them to a lengthy, discerning selection process to create a Haze that finishes faster with improved yields, but doesn't compromise the true haze high.

Like most hazes, Dutch Haze is still best suited to indoor or greenhouse grows, but the flowering time has been considerably reduced, finishing after 9–11 weeks of flowering or at the beginning of November in greenhouse gardens. Dutch Haze plants are robust, with good resistance to mold and spider mites, allowing gardeners to cultivate with greater success than most hazes. However, they still have a tendency to get large, and require size management. This strain yields 400g to 500g per square meter, even with the shorter flowering phase. This is a generous crop by sativa standards and a boon for haze gardeners.

The Dutch Haze high captures all of the uplifting intensity that haze enthusiasts crave. The smoke is rich and smooth with the distinct herbal flavors and smells of Haze perfuming the air with its incense. The movement into the high is a seamless experience in which everyday stresses seem to fade into the background and a heightened joyous awareness of living floods the senses. Gardeners who love Haze will recognize the genuine haze high, and also have a more gratifying experience during the growing process.

S

clear, soaring

smooth and hazey

63–77 days

♀ sativa haze x ♂ haze/mostly sativa

400–500g per m²

greenhouse

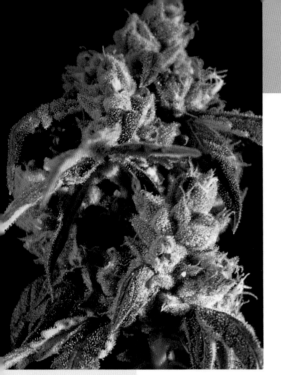

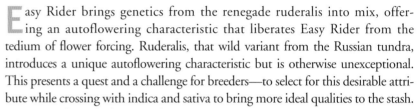

Easy Rider
Coffeeshop Classics by Ceres Seeds

 body stone

 acrid, earthy

 45 days

 ♀Dutch indica x ♂ruderalis

 14g per plant

 SOG

Easy Rider brings genetics from the renegade ruderalis into mix, offering an autoflowering characteristic that liberates Easy Rider from the tedium of flower forcing. Ruderalis, that wild variant from the Russian tundra, introduces a unique autoflowering characteristic but is otherwise unexceptional. This presents a quest and a challenge for breeders—to select for this desirable attribute while crossing with indica and sativa to bring more ideal qualities to the stash.

Ceres undertook this quest by crossing ruderalis to a Dutch indica-dominant strain from the skunk line well-known for its classical taste and high as well as its versatility in breeding. The result is a short, compact autoflowering plant that can grow successfully in conditions that would otherwise seem impossible: high in the mountains, high up in northern latitudes, or in conditions with lousy lighting or light pollution that would make a 12-hour dark cycle unfeasible. Since it is a cross, there is a chance that one or two plants will be indica-dominant, lacking the ruderalis autoflowering trait and waiting for the light cycle to flower.

The compactness of the Easy Rider plant make it suitable for small spaces and growing the plants close together, giving each about 6 square inches of space. Each plant only yields about a half-ounce, but yields are often still substantial due to the number of plants that can fit in a small garden. Easy Rider looks like a dwarf indica, with thick jade-colored leaves and small but solid buds. This is a 'bud on a stick' plant, surrounded by a lion's crest of minimal foliage so that sea of green gardening is a natural choice, and manicuring is a breeze. At finish, this plant is only about 2 feet (60 cm), which is a nice stealth quality. This modest plant can hide below a picket fence, banister, or balcony ledge. To add to its clandestine qualities, Easy Rider can be planted very early in the year and finish when other varieties are barely halfway through their growth cycle. The short season allows Easy Rider to serve as stash while the rest of the garden grows. Its sturdiness in colder temps also make it a good second crop, because it beats the rain in temperate climates and finishes before mold or bugs can settle in. An entire cycle can be completed start to finish in 60 days.

At finish, Easy Rider gets dark green, and the hairs turn a burnished copper-brown. Easy Rider is low on smell, both when growing and even when drying or being handled. The quality of the smell will depend on whether it was grown indoors or out, but its modest smell is a pungent, slightly acrid indica odor. This follows through in the flavor with an earthy depth and sour acerbic bite. The front flavor will cause a slight mouthwatering effect. Easy Rider's flavor is decent, but not remarkable. The high is a clear headed indica body stone. It does not induce the sleepy eye-droop look, but it is better suited as a sleeping aid than a party favor.

Funxta'z Purple Cali Kush
Don't Panic Organix

The Funxta'z Purple Cali Kush is an indica-dominant hybrid that blends a lanky OG Kush father with a mother Grand Daddy Purple indica from the wine regions in northwestern California. The OG Kush is a triple inbred cross (IBX) of an inbred line (IBL) of Kush. It is a more sativa-dominant strain with an enviable kush high. The purple mama is a hardy and stout plant that infuses the kush flavors with the purple tones of grapes and tartness of berries.

This West Coast Cali plant was bred in the inland desert regions of southern California, and it is very stable in dry or desert conditions. The FPCK does well in hydro or soil and delivers the best yield when topped and allowed to form several lilting limbs. As they mature, about half of the plants form lengthy branches like its OG Kush father, while the other half stay fairly stout and compact. Both types have very even growth, with more symmetry than most Christmas trees.

Funxta'z Purple Cali Kush is adapted to thrive in its home environment, making it very tolerant to overly warm temps and highly resistant to molds, mildews, and mites. After the fifth week of flowering, the buds dense up considerably, and the majority go fully chromatic, with strong deep purples that range into blue. Others will only form tinges of color while deepening to a vibrant green. All FPCK plants twinkle with a glow of heavy resin. The colas are wide and compact, often taking on a crown shape.

The FPCK high is a relaxed, yet energetic, happy high that creeps up progressively for the fifteen minutes after inhale and tends to linger for hours. Lightweight users should take care not to indulge too heavily at first, allowing the full effects to be revealed before proceeding. The initial high of Funxta'z Purple Cali Kush is great for concentration and motivation. It feels like the cleaning lady just tidied up inside your head, dusting out any cobwebs and leaving things with a sparkling clarity and orderliness that inspires productivity or excitement. This initial feeling fades to a mellow enjoyment, making it good for social activities or concerts where the beginning of the night is full of lively energy that naturally fades to a more casual mood. Medical users who treat depression or seek an energy boosting effect will enjoy this variety.

 60/40

 heavy creeper

 berry-grape diesel

 56–63 days

 ♀ Grand Daddy Purple x ♂ triple backcrossed OG Kush

 50g per plant indoor
500g per plant out

The Story of Funxta'z Purple Cali Kush
The Funxta
Don't Panic Organix

My varieties include the name "Funxta'z" because in my southern California home, I am known by this nickname in connection with my genetics work for a cannabis collective. I am passionate about creating high quality organic cannabis and helping the many patients who benefit from its effect. I discovered that breeding was very personally satisfying for me. In the beginning, I wanted to see if I could create a stable strain of high quality cannabis. I never expected to witness the diversity of the cannabis genus that I have seen. To this day, I am still blown away by the varieties that are possible and strongly alive. I want to bring forth New World techniques with brand new hybrids, and I always hope to find that 'special' genotype that gives back something to the community of cannabis patients and cannabis fans who have guarded the survival of this plant and its amazing healing properties.

In my opinion, Funxta'z Purple Cali Kush has something special to offer. Kush origins are often a source of confusion. This variety comes from the Chem/Diesel lines in California, not the landrace Hindu/Master Kush lines more common to European strains. The purple comes from the Grand Daddy Purple strain, giving a strong coloration at harvest and influencing the flavor, which to me is the essence of purple.

This strain was developed because patients were interested in rejuvenating a beloved Grand Daddy Purple mother plant that was aging. As a result, the clones were giving suboptimal yields. I was already developing seeds from an IBL OG Kush line for myself, and in that breeding work, I discovered a male that produced amazing progeny. Crossing this male with the Grand Daddy Purple mother restored the quality, vigor, and yield to a highly desirable plant.

Since my first attempts at breeding, I have learned so much about the plant kingdom and cannabis, and I've also learned so much from them. My advice for any budding growers and breeders out there is to study, learn, teach, don't discriminate, and go out of your comfort zone. Feed your mind with knowledge and learn from the unknowing. I couldn't call myself a cannabis breeder if I only worked on one variety in life. Cannabis should be a source of generosity, never a source of greed. I started this endeavor from my own joy in the process, but now my joy comes from being able to produce varieties that others need and want. I'm humbled by this plant and also glad that my work allows me to be a force for good in the lives of many patients.

G-Bomb
Big Buddha Seeds

From the underground networks of the UK arose a cutting that became the infamous "G," also known as G-Force. G's origins are unknown, but it has been making the rounds since the early 1990s. Rumors or educated guesses as to its composition have included Sensi's G-13 indica and Flying Dutchmen's spicy Pot of Gold, but these are unverified. Such guesses are based on the qualities that G shares in common with superstar Dutch indicas—a hardy and vigorous dark indica growth pattern, a unique effervescent quality, and a decidedly spicy hash taste.

When G-Force made it into the hands of Big Buddha, it was considered worthwhile to develop. Big Buddha feminized G by crossing it with a reversed G clone father, resulting in all-female, all-G strain, the G-Bomb. As a hefty indica, G-Bomb is a high yielding plant that forms gigantic colas the size of one's forearm. This plant likes to form a dense and impressive main central bud, making it a very solid choice for sea of green setups. If sea of green is unappealing, not to worry. Over many years, this strain has been grown in just about every common method from screen of green, big pots, hydro, coco, you name it—and its solid indica diligence leads it to perform admirably across the board. As such, it is a good plant to build up a beginner's confidence.

G-Bomb loves to be fed well and eats heavily. Indoor plants finish in 8–10 weeks, and outdoor plants can be harvested at the end of October. A little temperature variability is all right as long as the weather stays above freezing. G-Bomb maintains a steady monochromatic green, even when the nights turn cool. These plants also stay pretty short; at maximum outdoor sizes, they are still under the 6-foot mark (around 1.8 meters) at finish. Certainly size matters, but the right kind of size—not plant size, but bud size! This is where G-Bomb cashes in, delivering outdoor yields of up to 900 grams (nearly 2 pounds) per plant.

The G-Bomb aroma has been best described as dank lemony hashish. The citrus bite and an edge of spice will come through in the flavor. G-Bomb is a deep stone, with sedative potency. It is a great addition to the medicine stash of chronic pain sufferers, insomniacs, or others who want the soothing effects of a heavy, slow-release body indica.

I

sleepy, body stone

lemon hash

56–70 days

♀G x ♂reversed
G clone

400g per plant in
1000g per plant out

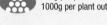

SOG

Green House Thai

Green House Seed Company

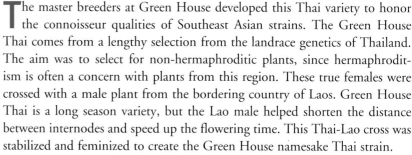

S I   85/15

cerebral, introspective, energizing, clear

spicy almond, cinnamon, sandalwood

98–112 days

♀Thai x ♂Laotian

500–600g per m²

The master breeders at Green House developed this Thai variety to honor the connoisseur qualities of Southeast Asian strains. The Green House Thai comes from a lengthy selection from the landrace genetics of Thailand. The aim was to select for non-hermaphroditic plants, since hermaphroditism is often a concern with plants from this region. These true females were crossed with a male plant from the bordering country of Laos. Green House Thai is a long season variety, but the Lao male helped shorten the distance between internodes and speed up the flowering time. This Thai-Lao cross was stabilized and feminized to create the Green House namesake Thai strain.

Green House Thai is characteristic of strains originating in tropical paradise locations. It is a tall sativa with long, slender lime-green leaves and impressive branching. The extended lower branches grow almost parallel to the ground, making it a very space-demanding plant. Green House recommends growing this strain under conditions that allow it to be grown to full size in order to achieve good production. Trying to harness this plant to a smaller stature works against this plant's nature and will diminish results. Growing in a screen of green system offers enough space for the plants to spread out to full potential, and leads to a uniquely pleasing stash.

This plant is for the sativa connoisseur, the gardener with some experience, or the patient beginner who wants to experience an authentic Thai strain. The flowering time is over 14 weeks, and depending on the environment, may take up to 16 weeks to truly ripen to its full spectrum of cannabinoids and terpenes.

Green House Thai can be grown in either hydro or soil. When grown within its homeland, this plant performs very well outdoors, but the long grow season limits outdoor growth to the equatorial region. Nights must stay above 15 degrees Celsius (about 60 degrees F). This variety also needs proper beauty sleep to flower properly, with a strict regimen of the 12/12 photoperiod and no light pollution. While the light and temperature conditions are exact, Green House Thai is not a very demanding plant when it comes to feeding. An EC of 1.7–1.8 will satisfy all her needs. Because of the long flowering time, it is advised to keep the nitrogen at good levels until the 4th or 5th week of flowering, or the plants will yellow prematurely.

In the right garden, one that can ensure the necessary conditions and the lengthy season, the Green House Thai pays off with some highly introspective headstash. The flavors and aromas are delicate, nutty, and incense-like, with flourishes of sandalwood spice, cinnamon, and almonds. This strain will satisfy those who like marijuana for its mind-opening qualities. It is ideal for meditation, yoga, or any creative moment outside of the social sphere. It is also a very nice morning smoke because of the mild, but long lasting effect on the body.

Headband
DNA Genetics/Reserva Privada

Imagine, if you will, throwing caution and all fashion sense to the wind, and donning a headband à la John McEnroe in the early '80s or Luke Wilson in the Royal Tennenbaums—or for the ladies, Olivia Newton-John aerobics-video style. The Headband is like a reassuring little brain hug, and its presence may bring a heightened awareness of the gray matter. Imagine a strain that, when smoked, mimics that feeling, moving rapidly from the front of the mind to the back, easing anxiety while inducing awareness. Now you have the idea.

The Headband is a brilliant case of reverse engineering by DNA Genetics. A choice, unidentified strain nicknamed the 707 Headband was making the circuit and gaining attention for its combination of potency and dank flavor. DNA breeders made some educated guesses about the parents of the 707 Headband, and then worked on recreating a strain from scratch that mimicked the 707's superb qualities.

This Headband's Sour Diesel/OG Kush combination brings together many admirable qualities from its already notorious parent strains. This is an agreeable squatty, bushy plant that makes the most of the available space. In the vegetative phase, it grows fast and spreads wide when allowed to go au naturale, producing many tops and an even canopy with minimal coaxing. At maturity, the size roughly doubles. This plant does not grow as tall as Sour Diesel or as stretchy as the OG Kush, and is less picky about the nutrients. Straight out of the gate, Headband is very pungent and colorful, taking a pinkish turn around the 4th week and gaining a wow factor with photo-worthy tones of blue, purple, and deep dark red in the last two weeks of ripening.

When finished, the Headband has great bag and head appeal. Its uniquely enjoyable fuel-sour taste makes it memorable. Soil does the best job in bringing out the flavor, but this plant produces good yields of high-grade medicine in coco, hydro, or other soilless methods so long as the plants are flushed with pH-balanced water for two weeks prior to harvest. The high is not too overpowering, and lasts a long time, making it a good utility daytime smoke. Headband is good for reducing anxiety. The beginner or hobby medical grower will find that this plant cooperates in the garden and delivers high quality yields.

3rd place, 2009 Cannabis Cup, coffeeshop category.

 70/30

 mellow, relaxing

 fuel-sour

 63–70 days

 ♀ Sour Diesel x ♂ OG Kush

 500–600g per m²

 SOG

Headband Story
DNA Genetics

The Headband name was actually inspired by an orphan strain of unknown parentage making the rounds about town and eventually making it to marijuana communities around the globe. This mystery strain, called the 707 Headband, was creating a stir with its combination of high-end features. It was a clone-only strain whose origins were unknown, and no one seemed to know the parentage. It was clear why people liked the 707 Headband: the fuel-like flavor was great, reminiscent of the Diesels with some Kush overtones. When the connoisseur breeders at DNA Genetics got a taste, they decided to put their powers of discrimination to work. In their estimation, 707 Headband tasted like a cross of OG Kush and Sour Diesel.

The OG Kush and Sour Diesel had both originated as great finds from bag seed, but the Headband had no seed to work with. DNA did not have any 707 genetics as seeds or clones to work from. Instead they put their expertise to work in breeding, using what they thought would best mimic the 707 Headband's genetics. The DNA Genetics Headband is only a form of flattery to its namesake, the original 707. The DNA Headband was created by reversing the OG Kush to pollinate the Sour Diesel. Next DNA breeders selected from the cross in order to produce the closest match to the 707 they could muster. People who smoke DNA Headband overwhelmingly agree that its flavor, look, smell, and density are a near-exact twin of the original 707. The pinkish color of the nuggs will also dazzle and amaze. Headband won 3rd place at the 2009 Cannabis Cup.

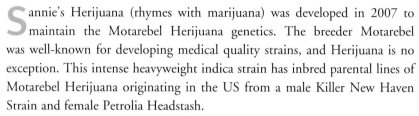

Herijuana
Sannie's Seeds

annie's Herijuana (rhymes with marijuana) was developed in 2007 to maintain the Motarebel Herijuana genetics. The breeder Motarebel was well-known for developing medical quality strains, and Herijuana is no exception. This intense heavyweight indica strain has inbred parental lines of Motarebel Herijuana originating in the US from a male Killer New Haven Strain and female Petrolia Headstash.

The Herijuana plant starts low and branchy and develops to an open-structure bush with vertically reaching branches and a leaf structure that reveals the sativa side of the strain. Herijuana buds, however, are true indica in form, growing many individual buds that are as dense as golf balls. Growers will find this plant an agreeable partner in the garden. She forgives brief extreme temperatures and shows resilience to other minor variations in conditions. Sannie's recommends organic fertilizers and a screen of green setup for maximum yields, although this plant can also be tamed to a sea of green setup with 16 plants per square meter.

Sannie's Herijuana has a larger node distance than the typical indica, making manicuring less intense. When flowered at about 2.5 feet (30 cm) it increases in size by about 1.5 times to reach a little over 4 feet (1.2 meters) at finish. The individual buds become very compact and resin covered, challenging some grinders with their density.

Growers will be eager to witness the formation of Herijuana's trichome-dense, ball-shaped buds. The smell is hashy and incense-like, and the taste is smooth with light sandalwood and dark coffee essences. This variety has become well-known among medical users for its strong and effective indica action. When smoked, the Herijuana reveals itself quickly in an intense, deeply physical and long lasting sedative stone. This is not a buzz for a lighthearted social evening or a neophyte smoker. For those seeking muscle relaxation or relief from insomnia, Herijuana holds much promise.

 80/20

 couchlock, intense, stoney, eyedroop

 coffee, dark, fuel, sandalwood

 49–56 days

 ♀♂ Motarebel Herijuana IBL

 400–500g per m²

 SOG

Himalaya Gold

Green House Seed Company

calm, stoney, munchies

dark coffee, chocolate

55–65 days

♀ Nepal x
♂ North India

100–200g per plant in
750–1000g per plant out

The Himalayan mountain range separates the Indian subcontinent from the Tibetan plateau. It is home to the planet's highest mountains, stretching across six countries with its dramatic contrasts of icy peaks and alluvial plains. This region, not far from the proposed origins of cannabis itself, is home to some fine landrace cannabis strains. The parents of the Green House Himalayan Gold originate in the Himalayan-bordering countries of Nepal and North India. These combined indica strains produce a fast growing plant with choco-smelling buds and a strong mellow high.

Himalayan Gold is well adapted for indoor or outdoor environments and can be finished by the end of September in south Europe when started in March. This rapid grower is very branchy, so much so that untamed branches tend to compete with the main cola. The Himlayan Gold plant works best as a trained multi-branch plant or in a screen of green setup; sea of green limits its potential.

Himalaya Gold's buds are elongated cattails, with a tight structure of indica chunkiness. These plants can become impressively large and prodigious yielders. Indoor plants tend to finish at around 4–5 feet (1.2–1.5 meters), but outside, they become giant bushes or small trees, getting as tall as 8 feet (2.5 meters). The chocolate aromas of this plant carry over in the dark flavors of its buds, with sweet and spicy edges of coffee and a hint of pepper, wood, and floral sweetness.

This all-indica treasure is stoney pot that hits the legs before it reaches the head. It has the potential to be a lazy, couchlock, snackfest buzz. It may bring out or enhance your inner procrastinator, so better to smoke when putting off until tomorrow is truly an option. Take pleasure in the relaxing bodily effects. This is a fun strain for playing videogames—the meditative, puzzle Tetris type, not the shoot 'em up variety. Because of the easy growing characteristics, tempting aroma and flavor, and potent effects, this strain is great for medical users looking for body effect, including those with MS or insomnia. Himalayan Gold can also really dial down the stress level.

Iranian Autoflower
Greenthumb Seeds

Iran is also widely known as Persia. This home to one of the world's oldest known continuous major civilizations has a long history with cannabis, and in particular with hashish, including tales that date back a thousand years. The country of Iran is roughly the size of the UK, or slightly bigger than the state of Alaska. It is southeast of Kazakhstan and Russia, two countries believed to be the birthplace of autoflowering strains. Iran has coastline along the Caspian Sea in the north and the Persian Gulf in the south, but is probably more known for being sandwiched between Iraq and Afghanistan. Much like these neighbors, Iran has much mountainous terrain, which turns to desert as one moves south and east.

Dr. Greenthumb's Iranian Autoflower strain is an all-indica strain with parents from the rugged terrain of Iran. It was developed for outdoor use in temperate climates. This lush green plant will grow anywhere, and finishes in just 90 days from start to finish. The Iranian Autoflower is compact, growing between 3–4 feet in most gardens, although it can reach heights of 5 feet at maximum. This variety tends to keep branching minimal and focus most of its energy on developing a single dominant cola.

This plant can finish in 3 months from seed to harvest, spending about half of that time in flowering. Since this is an autoflowering strain, the plants shift into flower development without strict light cycles, making it an easy plant to grow outdoors. Multiple harvests are possible from spring thaw to the first freeze of late autumn, and the lack of light requirements allows harvesting to occur in months during which outdoor harvests are uncommon, reducing many of the threats created by a more predictable schedule.

In addition, these plants are highly resistant to cold weather and only have minimal smell while growing. When combined with potential off season harvesting and compact size, they offer an impressive stealthiness for outdoor growers.

Iranian Autoflower buds form tight dense nuggets that take on golden hues as they cure. Average per-plant yields are 4–8 ounces. Iranian Autoflower reflects the long hashish tradition of its native region. In a side-by-side comparison, testers equated this all-indica strain's potency to White Widow and OG Kush. The deep earthy tones bring out flavors reminiscent of hashish, and the smoke has strong narcotic and pain-relieving qualities that lead card carrying med-users to ask for it by name.

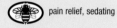 pain relief, sedating

 hashy, earthy

 40–50 days

 ♀Iranian x ♂NA S1

 100–200g per plant

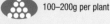

 SOG

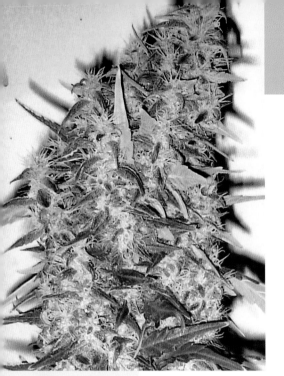

Jack F6
Sannie's Seeds

J ack Herer has become a classic strain known for its freshness and uplifting effects. The original Jack Herer variety combined a multiple-hybrid Haze with a sativa-indica Skunk. Sannie's Jack was developed to create a consistently sativa-dominant Jack Herer variety. Both parents come from inbred lines of Sannie's Jack.

Sannie's Jack F6 develops like a real sativa, with thin leaves and fast growth. It is advisable to not vegetate these ladies for too long since they continue to grow for 4 weeks after the 12/12 lighting switch. While they do shoot up quickly, Sannie's Jack F6 is not a branchy plant and tends to form a big main bud, making it suitable to a sea of green method. Nine plants per square meter are recommended for maximizing space without overcrowding. Screen of green growing techniques also work well.

Sannie's Jack F6 forms big foxtail buds that build up a heavy coat of trichomes. The buds are compact and powerful, like a bodybuilder's upper arm. These colas require support structures to keep them upright. The foliage stays an intense green during flowering. Average yields in a well tended garden range around an impressive 600 grams (over a pound) per square meter.

These translucent crystal-dense buds produce a clear, up high that comes on steadily and has a high ceiling, continuing to build over a long period of time.

The citrus tones are strong but not aggressive or overly acrid, leading to a very light, smooth smoke. Those who like a psychedelic leaning, euphoric buzz that lends itself to creative activities will find this variety delivers an especially pleasant experience.

 S

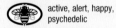 active, alert, happy, psychedelic

 citrus, fresh, spicy

 84–98 days

 ♀ Sannie's Jack F5 x ♂ Sannie's Jack F4

 500–750g per m²

 SOG

Long Live the Hemperor, *Jack Herer!*

By Bonnie King

"Because of one man's inspiration and stubborn refusal to accept anything less than legal cannabis, the movement has excelled beyond expectations."

Jack at the Seattle Hempfest.   Photo: Subcool

When Jack Herer spoke about hemp, everyone listened. A devoted cannabis warrior Jack unwaveringly believed that the cannabis plant, a renewable source of fuel, food and medicine, should be legal to grow and consume. He was outwardly dismayed with the US government, which he said hid the facts from American citizens. His book *The Emperor Wears No Clothes* was originally published in 1985 in order to make this unknown information widely available. It became the seminal book on the history of hemp and marijuana prohibition.

Now in its 11th edition, this book is considered a "Bible" of cannabis facts, and continues to be used as an essential research tool and catalyst in the advocacy to decriminalize cannabis. Everyone in the know has heard of it, read it, shared it, or referred to it in the debate over the merits of this plant. In fact, many of the most widely circulated arguments touting the benefits of cannabis entered the cultural consciousness with Jack's book. He soon earned the nickname "the Hemperor."

"Jack was basically on a book tour for 30 years," said Ed Rosenthal, worldwide authority on marijuana. "Many don't recognize that hemp is where it is because of Jack. He worked for this, and now it's happening: hemp is an available product, and prohibition is on its way out."

The Beginning

Jack spent the early 1970s in Venice Beach, California, where he opened two head shops. In 1973, he published his first book, *G.R.A.S.S.* (*Great Revolutionary American Standard System*), and met his friend and mentor Edwin M. Adair, aka "Captain Ed." Captain Ed changed Jack's life, bringing enlightenment to

Jack in his younger days. Photo: courtesy Jeannie Herer and Nicki Duzy.

what Jack had already learned about the far-reaching benefits of the hemp plant and sparking the flame that never dimmed from that point forward.

Jack and Ed Rosenthal

"Once he had this inspiration, the "aha" moment, everything changed," Ed Rosenthal said. "Jack saw the relationship with marijuana and hemp—that they had a similar destiny: if one is outlawed, so is the other; if one is legal, so will be the other. He had a profound understanding of the intricate connection between the medicinal herb and the industrial plant that required they be addressed as together."

In 1974, when Jack was 34, he and Captain Ed made their famous pact. In Jack's own words: "We swore to work every day to legalize marijuana and get all pot prisoners out of jail until we were dead, marijuana was legal, or until we turned 84 when we could quit. We didn't have to quit, but we could." Over the years, Jack and Ed had renewed their pledge several times. True to their word, they worked together on the issue until Captain Ed's untimely death at age 50 from leukemia in 1994.

The last time Ed and Jack renewed their pledge, Ed was in the hospital and it would be only days until he passed away. After Ed's death, Jack continued with their mission and lived on to fulfill their pledge. Ending marijuana prohibition and releasing victims of the drug war from jails and prisons were Jack's highest priorities for over forty years.

Jack Herer shouted his message from the rooftops, becoming the most well-known hemp activist in the world.

A Man and a Mission

A gregarious, bombastic man, Jack left an impression with everyone he met. As an activist he was a force to be reckoned with. Jack would take on a whole room full of naysayers and come out ahead. He insisted that hemp and cannabis groups alike support marijuana in all its forms, and he was happy to debate the issue. He once chided the Hemp Industries Association because he felt they were trying to separate the hemp cause from the more controversial marijuana issue in order to legitimate their cause. Jack felt they could not turn a blind eye to marijuana arrests and imprisonments and succeed. His message to hemp activists and entrepreneurs was this: "Until these people are out of jail, until this plant is legal in all its forms, you guys have a responsibility!"

There were those with whom Jack did not see eye-to-eye, but they found harmony by focusing on common goals. Chris Conrad, editor of the first edition of *The Emperor Wears No Clothes,* said the first time he met Jack, the two of them were arguing within minutes. "If you never got mad at Jack, and Jack never got mad at you, then you probably didn't know Jack very well." Jack was a good friend and a good guy to have on your side. Certainly, he was a lot of fun to smoke marijuana with! He had an indisputable talent for bringing all sides to the table.

Some stoner lore tells of Ed Rosenthal and Jack being super critical of each other. Ed says this is categorically untrue. "It never got to anything like that. We had intellectual arguments only; we were never rivals. We were two co-revolutionaries working on different aspects of the same project."

Jack and Subcool share a bowl. Photo: MzJill

Ed Rosenthal openly disagreed with a lot of positions presented in Jack's book, and Jack liked a good debate. After one such jousting, Ed told him, "You know what Jack? All these things are technical, they aren't negating hemp. You're saying the government should let hemp on the market. So am I." They agreed on it and the debate was settled.

Jack Herer's mission was driven not by a desire for fame or fortune, but rather by his unyielding determination to end hemp prohibition and thus right a wrong that had unfolded from a distorted misdirection in America's political history. Like many, Jack understood that US policies on hemp and cannabis were illogical and even detrimental to the earth.

"It is the safest, smartest, best medicine on the planet," Jack said. "You'd have to be stupid not to use it!"

Many know Jack Herer's name not for his activism, but for a high-grade strain of cannabis from Sensi Seeds with sativa dominant characteristics, named in honor of Jack's work. It is a complex strain that requires some gardening talent to grow it optimally, yet people love it because of its mentally stimulating and uplifting high that is fresh with a peppery bite. In these qualities, it shares much with Jack Herer, the man. The Jack Herer strain has won several awards, including the 7th High Times Cannabis Cup, the "Academy Awards of Marijuana." It has also become a popular choice as a parent strain with its mix of old-school skunk and the ever-popular west coast haze. Because of its genetic diversity, many Jack variants have also emerged on the market, bringing out different facets of the cross. Some of latest can be found in this volume.

In his book Jack reiterates cannabis' low risk use, "A smoker would theoretically have to consume nearly 1,500 pounds of marijuana within about fifteen minutes to induce a lethal response."

The first cannabis advocate to offer the challenge "put your money where your mouth is," Jack offered a reward of $100,000 to anyone who could prove marijuana had killed a user. To this day, no one has tried to collect.

Jack was a good friend and a good guy to have on your side. Certainly, he was a lot of fun to smoke marijuana with! He had an indisputable talent for bringing all sides to the table.

Every year, Jack and his crew would travel thousands of miles making appearances, book signings, and speaking engagements at hemp festivals and other events. Jack met hundreds of people a day, and to all of them he had the same message: hemp will save the world.

Jack showing me his hemp boxers, 2008 Photo: Austin King

He was also a pivotal figure in the fight for medical marijuana. In 1996, Jack assisted Dennis Peron in the passing of California Proposition 215, leading the way in the medicinal marijuana legality. Ending prohibition was still a few giant steps away, but Jack was adamant that it was within reach—closer, with each educated voter.

Jack was very opposed to taxing marijuana and became more fixed in his position with age. However, he understood progress, and the sacrifices required for advancement.

In 2000, the Hemperor suffered a heart attack and a major stroke resulting in long-term rehab for ongoing speaking difficulties and loss of mobility on the right side of his body. He was back in action after three years. In May 2004, he revealed that treatment with the *aminita muscaria*, a psychoactive mushroom was the secret to his recovery and the subject of an upcoming book (yet to be released). Jack was back and going strong.

Jack's tireless efforts did not go unnoticed by the larger cannabis community. In 2003, Jack Herer was inducted into the Counterculture Hall of Fame at the 16th Cannabis Cup in recognition of his first book *G.R.A.S.S.* An award was established in his name in 2004 by Patient Alliance. The Jack Herer Award or "the Jack," is considered the Oscar of Cannabis Awards. It is awarded to patients, activists, and celebrity stoners who bring the truth to the people at the highest level.

By 2009, Jack was back in full swing. He was speaking more clearly and said he felt better than he had in years. On September 12th of that year, he was at HempStalk in Portland, Oregon, where he was anxious to discuss the medicinal success of Rick Simpson's Healing Hemp Oil, whom he expected to join on a European tour weeks later. He was enthusiastic about the future.

"The Hemperor" Jack Herer passed away on April 15, 2010, at the age of 70. He is survived by a worldwide circle of thousands of friends and fans.

Jack's life's work was a gift to all generations, creating the foundation of a more enlightened social consciousness, and an example of what one dedicated man can do when he puts his mind to it and his life into it.

A hug from Jack. Photo: Subcool

On that fateful day, Jack encouraged the audience at HempStalk to continue the fight, to see the current marijuana initiatives through to success, and to resist the temptation to agree to pay the government to use cannabis.

"I don't want to give the United States government one fucking dollar of taxes. I think they should go to jail for getting you and me and 20 million other people arrested for pot, the safest thing you can do in the universe!" he declared. It was more than his opinion, it was his mission.

After his well-delivered speech, Jack's collapse and sudden heart attack were a shock. He was rushed to Emanuel Hospital in critical condition. About a month later he was transferred to Avamere Rehabilitation Center where he made some progress, but was unable to fully recover.

Jack Flash #5
Sensi Seed Bank

Photo: Soft Secrets Magazine

Sensi Seed Bank has delivered many classic breeds to the marketplace including the beloved Jack Herer strain. The original Jack Flash strain was derived from Jack Herer genetics and possessed some of its qualities, but also introduced skunk characteristics that improved its ease for gardening. In Jack Flash #5, Sensi has further evolved this family, producing a feminized, sativa-dominant cross of the Jack Flash variety. Jack Flash #5's mother was a stand-out Jack Flash phenotype, with which this feminized strain was backcrossed in the next-to-last breeding step. The female "father" was a superb Skunk/Haze hybrid that was extremely resistant to intersexuality, making the chances of hermaphroditic qualities in its feminized progeny as low as in a regular female.

The Jack Flash #5 is more sativa influenced than the original Jack Flash. During flowering, this variety is more poplar tree than pine, with upward-angled branches that create height and lead to as much as a 200% size increase unless controlled. The hybrid "stretched-teardrop" leaves have a fat indica middle narrowing to thin sativa tips. Jack Flash #5's large, dense buds have hybrid features, first clustering, and then running along the branches to fill the internodal space. As they mature, the colas form oversized oval calyxes with profuse pistils and an amazingly dense resin coating. The tops of the main buds often have multi-point crowns caused by large calyxes growing on top of one another.

Jack Flash #5 is a happy, vigorous plant that handles a wide range of conditions with grace. Sensi recommends this strain for indoor grows. These large ladies like a decent nutrient supply and tend to be resilient to fungus and minor grow room miscalculations. This plant can be controlled well in a screen of green grow, or tamed to single main stems and grown as a sea of green as longs as clones are put into flower almost immediately after rooting, at 4–5 inches (8–12 cm) in height. The main concern for Jack Flash #5 growers will be height jumps, although this variety is not as unwieldy as typical haze-dominated strains. Outdoors, this variety finishes in time when grown within 40 degrees of the sunny equatorial belt, but it may be more challenged to ripen before cool weather sets in at latitudes above 45 degrees N.

Jack Flash#5 has skunk elements in its earthy citrus aroma and flavor that many will find enjoyable and tasty. Beyond the appeal of its vigor, which makes it suitable even for beginners to deliver great connoisseur yields, the Jack Flash #5 will win hearts with its long lasting and strongly cerebral,

 55/45

 active, thoughtful, warm, stoney

 earthy citrus

 55–75 days

 ♀ Jack Flash x ♂ Skunk/Haze hybrid

 50–100g per plant

 in preferred

 SOG

The Jack Flash Story

The original Jack Flash was derived from the Jack Herer strain that kept the "Jack" part of its title from its hemp crusading namesake. The "Flash" part of the name came from the very fast onset of her effect and stuck in part due to the Rolling Stones reference formed by the two words.

Jack Flash has been a popular classic. Back when the original hybrid was released, many seeds of the new crossbreed were test-germinated. One example was found to be a particularly outstanding sativa phenotype female. Sensi's founders and breeders made her into a mother and kept her for a long time to provide ongoing personal stash. As often happens with breeders' favorites, this elite individual became a prime candidate for reproducing a new seed strain in its own right—perhaps with a touch more Haze. A short time later, work began to develop the special Jack Flash mother into a stable strain.

When improvements in feminization allowed the creation of reliable all-female seeds, the original JF #5 mother was enrolled in the program. The stabilized end product was named in honor of the superb mother plant whose qualities the breeders had labored to preserve. The #5 part of the name also references the fact that, going back a few generations, there have been five very famous plants in JF#5's ancestry: Haze, Skunk #1, Northern Lights #5, Jack Herer, and the original Jack Flash.

sparkling high. The effects come on fast, leading with the head and filtering into an indica body-buzz that creeps up and lingers. Unlike some varieties, repeat smoking may refresh the head effects and stave off lethargy, but of course this only works up to a point. The indica stone is likely to prevail in high doses or when smoked throughout the day. Still, Jack Flash #5 is not prone to stupefy smokers, so it is suitable for chilling out with friends in easygoing social activities, and most medical users will find it to be a well-rounded addition to the stash.

Jamaican Pearl
Sensi Seed Bank

Jamaican Pearl brings the mellow high and pungent flavors of the Caribbean to more temperate growing climates. This mostly-sativa hybrid has a Jamaican cultivar mother, Marley's Collie. Marley's Collie most likely descended from old-world sativas of south India, but she's been living in Jamaica a long time now, and over the generations, she's been carefully selected and cultivated to nurture the pungent tropical fruit and breezy cerebral high that is trademark Jamaican.

Sensi Seed Bank chose a special Early Pearl male as the ideal pollen donor for keeping the magic, but speeding up the flower time a bit. The Early Pearl strain is well-known as a fast flowering and vigorous plant, yet its sweet, heady qualities also make it a neutral influence on the flavors and high characteristic of the Caribbean, allowing the flavors and high from the Marley's Collie to shine through.

Jamaican Pearl is a hardy plant that grows beautifully outdoors in climates both warm and cool, and even thrives as far north as 60 degrees N latitudes. This plant also thrives indoors, so long as gardeners follow the general rules for sativa success in indoor gardens: paying attention to height gains and taking care not to overfeed plants. It is an excellent choice for those who like to top and grow multi-stem plants, or for those with screen of green setups. The sea of green technique can also be used if plants are flowered when they are small and then pruned to slender columns. Plants can be forced when they are as short as 4 inches (10cm) and will still finish at 3 feet (1m) in height.

This robust strain forms tall, thick stems with branches that reach strongly upward. Jamaican Pearl colas are thick and spear-shaped, and some have a spikier top with impressively long, silky pistils that reveal its island heritage. Buds cluster down the branch, then bulk up, filling in gaps as they ripen to form colossal cattail colas. Indoor buds may pile more calyxes on top of ripe ones, but gardeners should not be fooled by these, harvesting when the body of the bud is ripe.

Jamaican Pearl has the luscious smells of fruit, with a strong and exciting spicy flavor at the finish. The increase in head-altitude is quite rapid yet its subtle clarity often causes awareness to lag behind; several minutes after being high, the fact that you are high suddenly dawns on you. This buzz brings on a sunny disposition that make it well suited for daytime, conversation, and fun outdoor activities. Unlike some sativa strains, Jamaican Pearl tends to hold up over time for regular smokers without losing its ascendant qualities.

 60/40

 high, clear, happy, creeper

 fruity spice

 55–75 days

 ♀ Marley's Collie x ♂ Early Pearl

 up to 100g per multibranch in 250–500g per plant out

 out preferred

 SOG

The Jamaican Pearl Story

Jamaica is home to sativas of astounding quality and potency, so it seems strange that Caribbean genotypes have been relatively rare in modern breeding. Part of the difficulty for breeders is hybridizing without losing the luster of mellow euphoria that conjures up island life.

Island strains are a bit mystical. The rhythms of island life in the tropics are different, with the immense force of the ocean and its calming pulse so near. The balmy, lush surroundings seem to invite a slower pace and a lower stress level. It is hard to disconnect all of these influences on one's psyche from the delightful and soothing qualities of island kind bud. This can sometimes make carrying the qualities of island varieties back to the mainland elusive. Yet it is clear that island varieties have a certain sparkle to them, and Sensi Seed Bank has spent years working on varieties that carry this quality back home.

After years spent developing the Marley's Collie mother strain, an exquisite exemplar of what Jamaican ganja has to offer, Sensi breeders then turned their attention to the project that would become Jamaican Pearl. The goal with Jamaican Pearl was to retain the calm yet upbeat island qualities of the high in a plant that could finish—and flourish—outdoors in a northern summer.

The cross with a select Early Pearl male was a clear favorite, with results that impressed Sensi breeders right away. Test growers also found they could produce consistent, powerful sativa-leaning plants in temperate climates and harvest a generous yield of buds with clear tropical qualities. The popularity and consistency among testers has led Jamaican Pearl to quickly rise as a quiet star among outdoor strains.

The philosophy at Sensi Seed Bank is one of great respect for the plant. Cannabis gardening takes patience, focus, and serendipity—all qualities to nurture and treasure in life as well. To all those brave protectors of this plant, Sensi says: keep the faith, endanger yourself as little as possible, and remember that local laws are easier to change than national ones. Grow your own if you can, and if you can't, do your best to support those who support cannabis freedom in the world.

Jock Horror

Nirvana

J ock Horror is Nirvana's twist on the family of strains that arose around the Jack Herer name. The mother is a Haze 19 x Skunk, a hazey hybrid cross of Holland and California strains. Jock's father is an old-school Northern Lights, a mostly indica plant taken from a 20-year stable Afghan x Skunk #1 cross whose line was preserved in the marijuana mecca of America's Pacific Northwest.

This strain plays with a composition familiar in the Jack strains that began when Sensi's multi-haze-skunk cross adopted the name of the legendary hemp activist. However, Jock Horror is its own original strain derived from the breeding work and the genetics collection of the Nirvana team. In this inter-pretation, Nirvana combines a sativa haze, hybrid Skunk, and indica Northern Lights in a three-way cross that is mostly sativa. Jock Horror is a stable strain that has become a classic offering from Nirvana since it was first introduced in the mid-1980s and remains a tried-and-true favorite among Nirvana's breeding team.

The Jock Horror plant forms a traditional pine tree with medium-thin leaves and dense buds that cascade into extended calyxes, arching in a long cylinder of goodness. Nirvana recommends growing Jock Horror in soil with organics for the best flavors. Sea of green setups are good for Jock Horror because it does not branch very much, but the branches it forms are long. Jock really likes conditions to be reliable in the growroom, but is not as difficult as other connoisseur sativas, and not as bland as more commercial strains. This strain really smells up the garden, gaining two-thirds of its total height during flowering. Outdoors, this variety finishes at the end of October. It can reach monstrous heights of up to 9–10 feet (3 meters).

Jock buds at finish are frosty and tight. The calyxes often form horn-shaped ends as they pile on the tips of the colas. This strain may be a jock, but on finish the smell is fresh and inviting. The taste is floral with a tangy sweet-sour haze edge. Jock Horror offers a classic sativa high, powerful and visual with a nice endurance. It is a good strain for going out dancing, enjoying time with friends, or just making something dull more tolerable and possibly entertaining.

 70/30

 balanced, blissful, long lasting

 pungent fruit haze

 55–60 days

 ♀Haze 19/Skunk x ♂Afghan/skunk

 350–450g per m²

 SOG

K-Train

Green House Seed Company

K-Train takes its K from the Kush, as in the Hindu Kush mountain regions of marijuana's homeland, the origin of its OG Kush father. The OG Kush, side of the family is indica-dominant, drawing on a long line of Afghani genetics. K-Train's "Train" comes from the notorious Trainwreck, a beloved California native originating in one of America's marijuana hotspots—Humboldt County. Trainwreck stood out even in this land of kind bud because of its soaring, highly creative yet smooth and lucid high. K-Train combines these two highly appreciated strains to create a K-O strain for left-brain activities. This is a fast strong, physical buzz with a creative edge.

K-Train performs adequately in a sea of green, but screen of green setups work better. These indica-dominant plants have short internodes yet rapid growth in hydro or soil, with think dense colas. Green House gardeners prefer this plant in a hydro setup with synthetic fertilizers and an EC up to 2.2. After flower forcing, this plant finishes in 9 weeks, or it can be successfully grown outdoors, where it can be harvested at the end of September in southern Europe.

K-Train is a "stoned to the bone" strain with a rapid onset and deep body sensation, making it suitable for passive activities that are stimulating to the senses, such as watching surreal movies or listening to great music. The Kush's dark, nutty, and earthy licorice tones hold the bass line with a fruity, berry-like melody formed from the Trainwreck influences. The aroma has a spicy sweet roast of pistachios or almonds, but the spice tends to fade to sweet in the afterburned flavor.

Medical uses for this strain range from treatment of depression and stress to conditions that benefit from strong body effects. Take a ride on the K-Train and find yourself transported to a more relaxing state of mind without ever leaving the comforts of home.

 mostly indica

 lethargic, stoney, intense, munchies

 berry & dark earthy licorice

 60–65 days

 ♀ Trainwreck x ♂ OG Kush

 1.1 g per watt

 SOG

Kandahar
Ministry of Cannabis

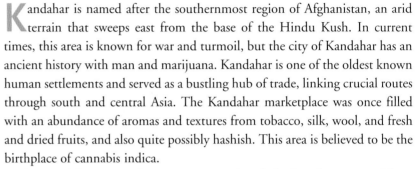

Kandahar is named after the southernmost region of Afghanistan, an arid terrain that sweeps east from the base of the Hindu Kush. In current times, this area is known for war and turmoil, but the city of Kandahar has an ancient history with man and marijuana. Kandahar is one of the oldest known human settlements and served as a bustling hub of trade, linking crucial routes through south and central Asia. The Kandahar marketplace was once filled with an abundance of aromas and textures from tobacco, silk, wool, and fresh and dried fruits, and also quite possibly hashish. This area is believed to be the birthplace of cannabis indica.

The Kandahar namesake strain is an indica hybrid with a pure Afghani mother and a father Afghani that has been crossed with a California Skunk to balance its characteristics. The Kandahar plant is a trademark indica—a squat, branchy plant with compact, tightly formed calyxes that evolve into pale green, resinous cones. The branches do not climb and stretch like its sativa cousin, but instead stay reserved and close, creating a narrow Christmas-tree growth profile.

Although optimal as a multi-branch plant, Kandahar can be tamed to a sea of green by a grower determined to use this technique. The leaflets are a paler green than one might expect from such a heavy indica, but they are thick with many leaflets. As Kandahar reaches maturity, the leaves may start to turn a bright yellow or may purple if the weather turns cold. Unlike some indicas, this plant can really soak up the PK, and she still takes 8–9 weeks to reach optimal ripening. Kandahar has good resistance to mold and fares well if the nights get a little nippy. Outside gardeners who plant in late July can harvest in the beginning of October. On average, indoor yields will range around 1 pound (500g) per square meter, or 14 ounces (400g) per plant outside.

If you have just sniffed plants with strong candy-sweet aromas, then Kandahar will not seem sweet by comparison. However, on its own, this variety captures the complexity of a street bazaar with sour-sweet fragrances that combine ripe fruit and dry forest muskiness. Once cured, the buds are nice tight nuggets with a woodsy and nutty taste and a hint of sandalwood. As they are burned they get the pleasantly warm fragrance of toasted nuts. The high settles deep in the body with a potential for couchlock intensity. Down tempo music, television, or other undemanding yet sensory activities will pair well with Kandahar's sedating qualities. It's all good—sit back, soak it in, and enjoy the satisfying sense of relaxation.

body relaxing, intense, narcotic

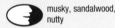
musky, sandalwood, nutty

56–63 days

♀Afghani x ♂Afghani skunk

500g per m2 in 400–500g per plant out

Killing Fields
Sannie's Seeds

The Killing Fields name originated from the expectation that this strain will yield fields of killer big buds. This strain was developed in order to infuse Sannie's Jack with sweetness, spice, and a kick, while shortening the flowering time. The mother combines a Blueberry sativa and the Killian strain from the US, whose name may have come from a well-known physician advocate for marijuana in the Seattle area. The father is a Dutch three-way Jack Herer family cross consisting of Skunk #1, Northern Lights #5, and Haze.

Killing Fields is recommended for indoor grows, using organic methods to heighten the candy spice qualities that are one of this strain's most notable features. This plant forms a big main bud with otherwise average branching.

Killing Fields develops like a typical hybrid during the vegetative phase. Once it enters flowering, the full sativa growth potential kicks in, leading to an impressively large pine tree of a plant. Gardeners may think the vegetative size is unimpressive, but it is a mistake to delay flowering. This plant will shoot up in size for a month after flower forcing, so it is important to anticipate the additional size requirements. Generous spacing is recommended for these plants, about 9 per square meter is appropriate for a sea of green. Screen of green produces maximum yields.

The Killing Fields leaves are large and thin, and vibrantly green throughout. The buds are large foxtails with tones that range by phenotype, with pink, blue, and green being the main types. At finish, Killing Fields delivers big dense buds that have a flashy, spacey, creeper high with a flavor of sweet-spicy overripe berries. This buzz is lucid and cerebral. It is highly functional for daytime or social activities, yet it can also be the type of high in which one can get caught up in the task at hand while remaining alert and engaged. A feminized backcross between a Killing Fields F1 and F2 selection is also available.

S

energetic, dreamy, mellow, physical

berry, candy, citric, spicy

77–90 days

♀Sannie's The One x ♂Sannie's Jack

500–600g per m²

SOG

Marijuana Cultivation in the Movies
Steve Bloom

Marijuana Makes an Appearance

When Reed Howes smoked a joint as Cowboy Dave in the 1929 western *High on the Range,* it was the first time marijuana appeared in a movie. Seven years later in 1936, *Reefer Madness* exploited society's fear of cannabis with lurid depictions of youth gone wild while stoned on "the weed rooted in hell." Originally titled *Tell Your Children,* this church-financed moral drama revolved around high school students who descend into a mad rampage of rape, murder, and suicide under the influence of cannabis. In its own day, this flick was practically unknown, but when rediscovered in the 1970s, it quickly gained cult film status. The incredibly inaccurate portrayal of marijuana's effects became comedic, if a little disturbing.

Marijuana would have to wait until 1969 to receive a fair shake in Hollywood, when the low-budget road movie *Easy Rider,* written by Peter Fonda, Dennis Hopper, and Terry Southern, became an instant classic. It won a number of awards, and is listed as one of the 100 best American movies by the American Film Institute.

Easy Rider captured the zeitgeist of a generation, which included a renewed appreciation for marijuana. The use of real pot in its scenes added to the movie's notoriety. The campfire scene in which hippie characters (Peter Fonda and Dennis Hopper) offer to "turn on" a straitlaced lawyer who'd come along for the motorcycle ride (Jack Nicholson) has become iconic. Rather than take a swig of whiskey, Wyatt (Fonda) instructs George (Nicholson) to "do this instead" as he passes him an actual joint. George lights it and tamely inhales. "You've got to hold it in your lungs longer, George," Wyatt advises. He takes another hit and soon joins Billy (Hopper) in a rambling conversation about UFOs.

"You're stoned out of your mind, man," Billy says, dismissing George's contention that he saw "forty of them flying in formation in Mexico."

Hopper, who died from prostate cancer on May 28, 2010, said about the marijuana use in *Easy Rider*: "We'd gone through the sixties and nobody'd ever seen drugs being smoked without going out and committing some kind of murder or atrocity."

With Hopper at the controls as both director and co-writer, he was the first to get marijuana right in the movies. *Easy Rider* pioneered a movie style as well as opening the door to a more benign depiction of marijuana use.

Up In Smoke

By 1978, Hopper had some company when Cheech & Chong came along with the uproarious *Up in Smoke*. From the opening scene when Man (Tommy Chong) and Pedro (Richard "Cheech" Marin) toke a huge joint in the front seat of Pedro's low-rider to the finale with a van made out of marijuana literally going "up in smoke," the dopey duo forged a new genre: the stoner comedy.

Cheech & Chong returned with *Nice Dreams* in 1981, crossing into new territory by featuring the first growroom in film history. The grow belongs to a gardener named Weird Jimmy (played by Jimmy Fame). Shots of the room show Jimmy's garden hidden from aerial views with a blue tarp. The plants aren't real. They're plastic or silk, but they stand tall with buds protruding as a humming electrical sound pervades the background.

"Hey, electric weed man!" Cheech says to Jimmy in greeting. Cheech is in a NORML t-shirt; Jimmy's wearing a *High Times* smuggler's plane shirt.

For years to come, buddy stoner movies—including *Bill & Ted's Excellent Adventure* (1989), *Half Baked* (1998), three *Friday* flicks (1995), two *Harold & Kumar* films (2004), and *Without a Paddle* (2004)—would follow the nutty formula of slacker dudes going on some sort of quest that generally revolves around marijuana.

Marijuana Drama

While the Cheech & Chong era introduced the hilarious stoner comedy, a more dramatic cannabis storyline only emerged in the late 1990s. These dramas told a different, often darker, story about marijuana, but it is interesting that they rarely revolved around any *Reefer Madness*-style dangers of actual marijuana use. Instead, most of these movies show how the criminalization of cannabis squeezes growers between the threat of a bust on one side, and the dangers of thieves, criminals, or shady characters on the other. Often, the burgeoning cultivation industry is at center stage, providing many opportunities to show a diversity of gardens, from greenhouses to outdoor grows to closet cultivation.

One of the first such movies, *Homegrown* (1998), is based on a story written by former Yippee Jonah Raskin and directed by Stephen Gyllenhaal. The film begins with three characters tending a large, outdoor guerrilla grow in northern California. Intrigue builds immediately when their boss is killed, leaving the operation in the growers' less-than-capable hands.

Although the harvest still consists of synthetic rather than real plants, *Homegrown* shows a more thorough insider look at marijuana cultivation, with scenes that incorporate drying and manicuring plants. This movie also makes the shift from generic marijuana to named marijuana varieties. In this case, Carter (played by Hank Azaria) describes the plants as "Northern Lights crossbred with Afghani." The bud in the rolling tray certainly looks real.

This movie also incorporates US cannabis culture, giving a snapshot of one of the infamous cultivation regions in the states, California's "Emerald Triangle"— known for its concentration of marijuana growers. *Homegrown* portrays the cannabis farmers of Humboldt County as ex-hippies and society dropouts whose grow operations are as much a lifestyle choice as a form of income, and often involve generations of the same family. These local farmers are fighting to keep organized crime and its mentality out of their businesses. The story also shows the importance of trust, and the uncertainty that arises when trust breaks down.

A decade later in 2008, Northern California once again served as the backdrop for a pot-themed drama. Darren Grodsky and Danny Jacob's *Humboldt County*

is a far better depiction of cultivation in the Emerald Triangle than *Homegrown*. The cinematography offers a vivid peak into this region, including a scene with a large outdoor grow among the redwoods.

At its core, *Humboldt County* is about relationships, especially those between fathers and sons. Father Jack (Brad Dourif) and son Max (Chris Messina) have different ideas about how to safely grow a crop. Family secrets intertwine with the threat of crop rip-offs and DEA raids to build a suspenseful story. The best insight on weed comes from Jack, in a monologue where he offers his philosophy for growing in such a risky environment.

"This herb has been part of human civilization since before it was civilized," Jack pontificates. "But it is currently illegal. I've lost too many friends over it. Since the

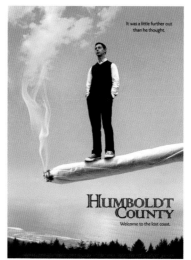

Mexicans have been coming across the border, the Feds have shifted their resources. We're nothing more than mom and pops, but that does not mean we can do what we want. It's a foolish man who underestimates his enemies. It's a stupid man who underestimates the Feds. After all these years I have 20 plants total, enough to get by. Any more than that and you're tempting fate. If we allow greed to enter into our lives, then we've destroyed the very thing we came out here for."

Stuart Birkin's *Cash Crop* came out in the same year as *Homegrown,* but was set on the other side of the country in rural Pennsylvania. In a community where family farmers are struggling to survive, several decide to band together and begin growing marijuana both indoors and amongst the corn stalks. But the DEA is onto them, and agent Becka Anslinger (clearly named for the original anti-drug warrior Harry J. Anslinger, who was from Western Pennsylvania) enlists the local sheriff (played by *Mad Men*'s John Slattery) to tour her around.

You never really see the crops in this film; instead, the focus is on the farmers' dilemma. Other movies will follow this lead, showing normal everyday people as cannabis growers. The farmers' motivations are noble, and it seems absurd to call them criminals. As the DEA witch hunt progresses through the film, even those enforcing the laws, including the sheriff, question the morality of doing so.

In 2000, Nigel Cole's *Saving Grace* would weave a similar story in a British setting. The main character, Grace (played by Academy Award nominee Brenda Blethyn), lives in a small village in England. After the death of her husband, she's having problems paying the bills on a huge estate. Grace must lay off the estate's gar-

dener, Matthew (played by late-night TV host Craig Ferguson, who co-wrote the film). In a desperate effort to save them both from financial ruin, Matthew shows Grace several scrawny plants he's growing in the nearby woods, and suggests they use the estate's greenhouse instead.

The cannabis greenhouse in *Saving Grace* is a marvel, like something out of *Little Shop of Horrors,* with odd lights, silver ductwork, and plants sprawling everywhere. Unlike *Cash Crop,* this movie shows plants and cannabis gardening close-up. One scene revolves around

cloning, with Grace and Matt dipping cuttings into a rooting compound then placing them in rock wool cubes. We also get some very specific strain information. Their plants are described as an indica-sativa hybrid, a combination of Purple Haze and Early Girl crossed with ruderalis (which should make them auto-flowering plants).

After several months, Grace produces one particularly monstrous plant. Though clearly synthetic, it's a beauty—the greatest fake pot plant to ever appear in a movie. Huge in every sense, the red and purple hairs stand up like antennas, and the dark green leaves glisten. Hung upside down to dry, the plants look more like ratty brown dreads than succulent green colas.

Saving Grace has its comedic moments, mainly in portraying the initiation of a naïve, middle-aged, middle-class woman from a small English village into marijuana cultivation and the cannabis trade. Still many of the plot's twists and turns rely on the necessity for secrecy from the local authorities, and the dangers involved in selling pot on the black market. While the drama builds, the tone stays light, and concludes with the entire cast dancing around giddily to the tune of "Witchcraft" as weed smoke wafts in the backyard. Cuckoo indeed!

Recent dramas include the 2006 movie, *Everything's Gone Green.* Directed by Paul Fox and written by Douglas Coupland, this movie is set in the popular growing region of British Columbia. Bored with his life, Ryan Arlen (*Road Trip*'s Paolo Costanza) decides to re-evaluate his options. His friend Spike (Gordon Michael Woolvett)

has a growroom tucked away in a walk-in closet at his dairy business. "I've got franchises in 25 basements across the city," he tells Ryan. "This plant here yields four pounds and sells for $10,000. Best smoke in North America, my friend." The indoor growroom shown in *Everything's Gone Green* is bustling and scientific, with lots of workers in lab coats, large umbrella shaped ballasts and rows of five-foot faux plants.

When Ryan discovers that his family is also involved in cultivation, the situation becomes more complicated and also humorous. The parents clearly see the marijuana laws as unjust. They believe that growing pot isn't "doing any harm to society," and ask "why don't [the cops] go after the real drug dealers?" Ultimately this film is about Ryan coming to terms with his own objectives.

Scary Mary Jane

For those who like thrillers, there have been a few notable cannabis films that will keep you on the edge of your seat.

British director and future Academy Award winner for *Slumdog Millionaire,* Danny Boyle brought us a nail biter in *The Beach.* Based on Alex Garland's 1996 novel of the same name, *The Beach* is set in Thailand on an idyllic island where a hippie community has found a home. While in Bangkok, Richard (Leonardo DiCaprio) is given a map to the island and arrives with two other travelers. Within minutes they stumble into a huge pot field. "This is what I call a lot of dope!" Etienne (Guillaume Canet) exclaims. Armed guards patrol the field and the trio barely escapes en route to "The Beach."

All is good until a new group with whom Richard shared the map shows up. They're not so lucky. "Dope Heaven" turns into a nightmare when they're killed by the guards. In the DVD commentary, Boyle blames marijuana's prohibition on their deaths as well as reveals that the large field (hundreds of plants) was actually hemp. "We grew all these plants," he says. "Many of them were stolen by people who thought they were dope. They probably were dried and sold to tourists as the real thing, ironically by locals. So we lost many of the plants in the process."

Another dark adventure is Alfonso Cuaron frightening 2006 sci-fi flick *Children of Men*. It's set in a dystopian 2027, 18 years after the last baby in the world was born. A rare pregnant mother needs shelter.

Theo (Clive Owen) works for the government and is enlisted by his ex, Julian (Julianne Moore), to help transport the mother, Kee (Clare-Hope Ashitey), to the Human Project. He makes several stops at the home of his aging friend Jasper (Michael Caine), who's tucked away in the woods.

Jasper has a large grow area with tall plants that are adjacent to the living room. "Dirty government hands out suicide kits and anti-depressants, but ganja is still illegal," he complains, while lighting a joint and passing it to Theo. "Taste that… cough?" Jasper instructs. "Cough?" "Yes, cough." Theo inhales and hacks. "Taste that?" Jasper asks. "Strawberries. This is Strawberry Cough!"

Why and how Cuaron and his screenwriters chose this particular strain is unclear, but it sure made Kyle Kushman smile—he had helped breed Strawberry Cough with New York friends in the late 1990s and later sold it to Dutch Passion.

Although marijuana is in many ways a side plot to this horrific and paranoid depiction of the future, its importance is clearly as a symbol of defiance against the system, and in a sense, a small piece of sanity in a world that has fallen into chaos.

Marijuana Mayhem

While 1998 gave us the dramas *Homegrown* and *Cash Crop*, it is also the year that Guy Ritchie's uber-violent *Lock, Stock and Two Smoking Barrels* came out. A British crime comedy, its pace and energy place it in the same genre with Quentin Tarantino's *Pulp Fiction* and Danny Boyle's *Trainspotting*. This highly quotable movie mixes marijuana with society's seedier elements, including gambling, gangs, and guns. The plot moves swiftly, taking several clever twists and turns along the way.

Set in London, several gangs case a growroom operated by a group of pacifists. "We grow weed, we're not mercenaries," Winston (Steve Mackintosh) explains. The plants, grown in hydro tubes, end up getting jacked several times amidst plenty of machine-gun fire. Again, we find growers beset on both sides, fighting against criminals while evading the authorities. By the end, it's unclear who's got the herb, but we do know who winds up with two very valuable rifles.

Despite marijuana's expansion in films to include specific cultivation processes and different types of gardens, almost all the marijuana you see growing in movies is not the real thing. The plants are generally made of out synthetic silk in China, just like the pot leaf leis that are so popular at rally events. One company, New Image Plants, sells six footers for $325 each and individual buds for $38 a piece. Their faux plants have been used on the TV shows *Weeds* and *Lost*, and in movies like *Leaves of Grass* and *High School*.

However, in 2002 the movie *High Times' Pot Luck* actually showed marijuana on screen. Its main character Frank (Frank Adonis) is a mobster who experiences a change in perspective after smoking weed with punk rocker Jade (Theo Kogan). Described as Cheech & Chong meet *The Sopranos*, *Pot Luck* follows a suitcase containing 20 pounds of weed around New York from the mules, to thieves, then to Frank to Jade.

When two mules visit a farmer in the opening scene, real plants are hanging to dry. "You're looking at the result of Cannabis Cup winning seeds," the farmer boasts. Before leaving, one of the mules hands the farmer a copy of *High Times*. "You made the centerfold again," he gushes.

More lighthearted than *Lock, Stock, and Two Smoking Barrels*, *High Times' Pot Luck* has the pace of a caper with the plot veering and turning as the suitcase changes hands. It ends at a pot rally in New York City where all of the principle characters show up and the contents of the suitcase are revealed to the delight of the crowd.

These marijuana mayhem stories presaged David Gordon Green's *Pineapple Express*, the top grossing stoner movie ($87 million at the box office) since *Up in Smoke*. This smash hit from 2008 relies on the fresh humor of Canadian writer and actor Seth Rogen and his writing partner Evan Goldberg, who also wrote *Superbad*.

The main character Dale Denton (played by Rogen) is kind of a loser, but in many ways, he's just an average dude. When he visits his dealer Saul Silver (James Franco) to buy weed, the ritual is pedestrian, and even kind of a boring prospect to him, like visiting a dull relative.

As it turns out, Saul is stocked with a hot new strain, Pineapple Express. "This is like if that Blue Oyster shit met that Afghan Kush I had—and they had a baby," Saul tells Dale. "And then, meanwhile, that crazy Northern Lights stuff I had and the Super Red Espresso Snowflake met and had a baby. And by some miracle, those two babies met and fucked—this would be the shit that they birthed."

They light up the famous cross-joint. "Just sit back and get ready to enjoy some of the rarest weed known to mankind," Saul hypes. "It's almost a shame to smoke it. It's like killing a unicorn....with, like, a bomb."

The real action begins when Dale, a process server, sees a murder take place. Freaked out, he tosses the joint of Pineapple Express he's smoking out the window of his car and races over to Saul's place. But because the weed is so distinctive, Dale thinks they'll trace the joint back to Saul. So Dale and Saul decide to run. Their flight is filled with stoner humor that compounds their problems. Every step along the way leads them to a slightly crazier interaction than the one before.

Eventually in their efforts to avoid the killer, they decide to go to the source, a huge warehouse in the middle of nowhere. Inside, there are rows upon rows of six-foot plants. "Look at all this weed, man," Saul says. "Granddaddy Purple, Purple Urkel, OG Kush!" In the end, Dale and Saul fight off all sorts of enemies as gunshots ricochet throughout the warehouse, which by the end goes up in smoke. These goofy stoners improbably transform into action heroes in order to save their own skins.

Since *Pineapple Express*'s box-office juggernaut, only one movie has followed its lead in combining stoner comedy with violent action. Intended for a 2010 release, Tim Blake Nelson's *Leaves of Grass* was postponed and may never come out in theaters, which is too bad because it has one of the best growroom movie scenes of all time.

Ed Norton plays identical twins, Brady and Bill Kincaid. Brady grows pot in Oklahoma, and Bill teaches philosophy at a prestigious Northeast university. The two brothers have little in common and haven't seen each other in years, but Brady concocts a scheme to get Bill to Tulsa, and he falls for it. Suddenly Bill has been sucked into Brady's operation.

The growroom setup looks like an amusement park ride. In the back of the room are rows of fake potted plants. In the front is a nutrient film technique (NFT) hydroponic system, with seedlings nestled at various key points in the plastic spiral tubing.

"I'm a sodium vapor, man," Brady says about the lighting. "You're looking at the motherfucking state of the art. They're all my special little children. You want to try some?"

It's the highlight of the movie, which like *Pineapple Express* becomes increasingly violent as it speeds to the climax.

By the way, if you get a chance to see *Leaves of Grass* and the plants look familiar, there's a good reason: They're same ones that were used in *Pineapple Express*.

Steve Bloom is co-author of *Reefer Movie Madness: The Ultimate Stoner Film Guide* and *Pot Culture: The A-Z Guide to Stoner Language & Life*. He publishes the popular marijuana news and entertainment website, CelebStoner.com. From 1988 to 2007, he worked at *High Times*.

Kushadelic
Soma's Sacred Seeds

Kushadelic brings out the delicious psychedelic side of the Kush family. This strain is Soma's cross of a California OG Kush and his special daddy haze. The haze daddy is a selection from Soma's intensive work with hybrid hazes, a G-13 Haze/Neville's Haze cross that has influenced many of his recent strains and beyond.

Kushadelic is a 50/50 hybrid, blending the hazier qualities of the sativa with the indica voluptuousness and density of the Kush. This plant begins the vegetative phase with full, picture-perfect leaves that balance indica/sativa influences. As it progresses through flowering, the leaflets elongate to a more slender sativa appearance by finish.

For most regions in the world, Kushadelic is an indoor variety, taking over 6 months from seed to finish outdoors, and a full 10 weeks in flowering under lights. Soma prefers organic soil methods with guano as fertilizer to bring out the best flavors and also to keep the most human-friendly, earth-friendly harvest, but this strain will also thrive when hydro methods are used. There are two phenotypes of the Kushadelic. One is more strongly sativa with a stretchier profile and a stronger haze effect in the buzz. The other is an indica pheno, which stays more squa in structure and reveals more kush influences in the final product.

Kushadelic is not a big brancher, but the plants respond well to being topped and will grow nicely as a multi-branch plants. They are also a solid choice for a sea of green technique, although the canopy may take some management for consistency. Indoor plants typically finish at 3 feet (1 meter), but when grown outdoors, these plants often reach heights over 7 feet (2.5 meters).

Kushadelic buds are large and sweet with an exotic marriage of the floral and earthy tones of the haze-kush combination. The high also brings together the potency of the kush with the happy clarity of the haze to cause a deep sense of repose and an introspective yet social attitude.

 50/50

 soaring, alert

 fresh floral haze

 70–80 days

 ♀ OG Kush x ♂ G-13 Haze

 25–50g per plant

 SOG

L.A.P.D.
California Bean Bank

L.A.P.D. stands for LA Confidential Purple Diesel, which incorporates the names of both parents for this strain while giving this strain an unmistakably left coast address. LA Confidential is a celebrity strain that made the rounds in the 1990s Los Angeles market and then became available through DNA Genetics. This parent is primarily OG Kush genetics, with its signature heavy indica hashiness, sweet spice-like flavors, and sultry, dreamy high that borders on the psychedelic. The Purple Diesel parent counteracts the lazy in the LA Confidential with a big burst of energy that may translate into physical activity or creative pursuits. The Purple Diesel is that jacked-up, clean-your-house-with-the-music-blaring weed that some people love, all wrapped in a slightly sour and purely pungent package.

When combined in the L.A.P.D., this 50/50 cross is a versatile multi-tasker. It does well indoors and out, but makes its best showing when greenhouse grown. L.A.P.D. also transitions well in many gardening styles, including soil or hydro gardens, in SOG or SCROG setups. It is particularly good for hot dry climates characteristic of the southwestern U.S. including southern California and also into Nevada, Arizona, and other hot dry states. Those in wetter or more humid climates will have to watch for molds since the bud formation is very tight. Although the L.A.P.D. plant tends to follow its indica half of its roots and stay on the shorter end of the scale, it will stretch greatly if kept too far from the light. Harvest times are fairly fast, finishing in as few as 7 weeks indoors or early to mid-October when grown outside or in a greenhouse. At ripeness, L.A.P.D. forms incredibly compact and dense, crystal-laden nuggets with interesting crimson and purple tints.

Yields of the L.A.P.D. are solid, with a typical harvest between 2.5–3.5 ounces (80–100g) per plant, or 300g per square meter in a sea of green. Outdoor yields max out at a little over a pound (600g) per plant, but CA Bean Bank favors the more concentrated effects of indoor grown L.A.P.D. over the mellower outdoor bud. L.A.P.D. is very heady, and begins with the Purple Diesel's up effects, but quickly settles into a much calmer and more sedate buzz. With light inhalation, it is an effective body relaxant; in heavier doses, it is seriously intoxicating. CA Bean Bank breeders say, "to protect and serve or to take you out—the L.A.P.D. can do both." Taste fans will enjoy this strain's sweet top notes of grape and pine carried with a rich earthy undertone and a little bit of pepper on the finish. Medical users may appreciate the strong body effects, which are good for stress, cramps, spasms, chronic pain, and fatigue.

 50/50

 strong headiness, physically relaxing

 earthy, pine, peppery

 50–60 days

 ♀LA Confidential x ♂Purple Diesel

 80–100g per plant in 450–600g per plant out

 greenhouse recommended

 SOG

Lemon Skunk
DNA Genetics

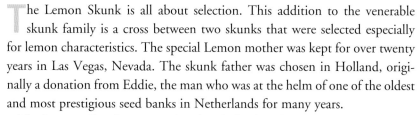

The Lemon Skunk is all about selection. This addition to the venerable skunk family is a cross between two skunks that were selected especially for lemon characteristics. The special Lemon mother was kept for over twenty years in Las Vegas, Nevada. The skunk father was chosen in Holland, originally a donation from Eddie, the man who was at the helm of one of the oldest and most prestigious seed banks in Netherlands for many years.

The Lemon Skunk is a sativa-indica hybrid with a slightly higher sativa ratio. It has sativa-hybrid characteristics, growing tall but with a high calyx-to-leaf ratio, making it easy to trim. The structure of the plant tends to be open, but can get somewhat bushy, so it works best as a multi-branch plant. Lemon Skunk fares well with moderate to heavy nutrients and doesn't mind the heat. The leaves are a medium to lighter green with medium to slender sativa style leaflets, and the buds also stay light green and form a profusion of orange hairs. At finish, this bud is dewy with crystalline resin. The Lemon Skunk strain takes 8–9 weeks to finish, but reaches its apex of sweetness if cut down between 50 and 56 days.

Lemon Skunk is a tasty sweet citrus bud for those who like a fresh fruity stash. The enjoyable sativa-leaning high boosts the senses, bringing on thoughtful reflection and heightened sensory perception. It may also boost the sense for a need to go spelunk through the fridge for some munchies. Fans of the fresh-citrus end of the cannabis flavor palate will understand why Lemon Skunk has won multiple awards, including a cup at Spannabis and a first place win for outdoor at the Highlife in 2007.

1st place, Spannabis, Indoor Hydro category 2008
1st place, *Highlife* Cup Outdoor category 2007
2nd place, IC420 Breeders Cup 2008
Winner, *High Times* Top 10 Strains of the Year 2009

 60/40

 fast onset, energetic

 pungent, lemon

 56–63 days

 ♀ skunk x ♂ skunk

 400–500g per m²

LSD

Barney's Farm

trippy, visual, euphoric

sweet, musky, earthy

55–65 days

Mazar x Skunk #1

600g per m²

in preferred

It doesn't take a detective to figure out how LSD got its name. This variety lets marijuana's freak flag fly, bringing out pot's most psychedelic qualities. The Mazar parent is a strain that was probably better known by name a decade ago when it was newer to the scene. Mazar has often been compared with the better known White Widow for the similarities in plant and bud structure and effects. Both strains are indica-sativa hybrids, although Mazar is more indica heavy, as suggested by the name, which references the presence of Afghani in the parentage and comes from the name of Afghanistan's fourth largest city, Mazar-e-Sharif.

Barney's Farm Seed Bank used these long established genetics in combination with the versatile Skunk #1 to create the LSD variety. These parents have passed along many of their strengths. LSD is a hardy, disease-resistant plant that thrives in nearly all reasonable growing conditions. These plants stay light to medium green with leaves that split the difference between sativa and indica thickness. Flowering takes 8 to 9 weeks. At first the LSD plant may seem dense with foliage, but the buds soon outshine the vegetation. LSD buds form slightly curved corkscrew triangles with large stacked calyxes and a profusion of burnished hairs. While plants remain fairly compact and can be staked or grown successfully in a sea of green, LSD also delivers satisfying yields as a multi-branch plant, often reaching 600 grams per square meter. When grown outdoors, LSD plants finish in mid-September.

The LSD flavor mixes a slightly nutty and earthy palate with a dank sweet muskiness. Best of all, LSD lives up to its name, delivering a vivid, euphoric experience that stands out from the typical indica stone. While the body high has depth, the strongest sensation is the super trippy psychedelia that will blow the cobwebs out of the corners of your mind. This strain is great in a stimulating environment. Music, food, and colorful imagery will all be enhanced under its influence. However, overindulgence or overly hectic situations may cause a sense of being overwhelmed so it can be good to stay somewhere that also offers a sense of comfort and safety. Medical users have recommended this strain for nausea, anxiety, depression, and headaches. LSD won the 2008 Cannabis Cup in the Indica Category.

Mandala #1
Mandala Seeds

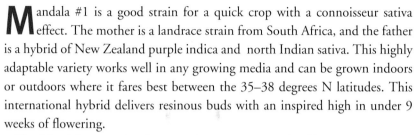

Mandala #1 is a good strain for a quick crop with a connoisseur sativa effect. The mother is a landrace strain from South Africa, and the father is a hybrid of New Zealand purple indica and north Indian sativa. This highly adaptable variety works well in any growing media and can be grown indoors or outdoors where it fares best between the 35–38 degrees N latitudes. This international hybrid delivers resinous buds with an inspired high in under 9 weeks of flowering.

The Mandala #1 variety has two phenotypes. One-third have a sativa structure and grow in a classic Christmas-tree shape, although the leaves resemble the indica-dominant phenotype, which grows more stout and forms a thick main stem. The indica pheno is shorter and branches close to the main stem, making it perfect for sea of green. Both conform well to screen of green methods or other forms of training. The Mandala #1 phenotypes grow peaceably alongside one another indoors. Harvesting and cloning this plant is simple given its hardiness and high calyx-to-leaf ratio.

For outdoor growers in northern climates where harvesting by the end of September is a priority, Mandala #1 is an excellent choice. This hardy hybrid has been grown successfully in latitudes between 35-38° N, even in difficult weather conditions in Canada, Switzerland, and Eastern Europe. The combination of robust landrace genetics produces early-flowering plants that beginners can grow. Mandala #1 is not fussy about feeding and does well with moderate feeding or with nothing but good horticultural grade potting soil to subsist on. Mandala Seeds always grows organically in soil and recommends these methods for those who want great flavors. One of their breeding goals is to ensure flexible and stable strains that can be raised indoors and withstand the stress of switching between artificial lighting and sunlight. It is possible to start your garden inside or in a greenhouse, and then move the plants outside for flowering.

As a young flowering plant, Mandala #1 has a perfumed woody-herbal fragrance when the stems are rubbed. Purplish leaf stems and light red stripes along shoots should not be mistaken for a nutrient deficiency. Despite the sativa dominance in the high, the bud structure is more indica-chunky, with a spear-shaped main bud of considerable length. The prime buds are coated with a thick layer of trichomes and glisten brightly with their magic promise. Some plants also develop beautiful dark purple calyxes during mid-flowering, a trait which they inherited from the New Zealand Purple Indica in the paternal line.

 sativa-dominant

 dreamy, uplifting, creative

 herbal fruity berry

 55–60 days

 ♀S. African Highland sativa x ♂indica/sativa hybrid

 450g per m² in 800–1200g per plant out

 SOG

The Mandala #1 high spreads in euphoric waves of creative inspiration. It may start dreamy and a little spacey, but quickly settles into a relaxed and motivated sensation, with no racing-heart or other unpleasant side effects. This strain has the sweet fragrance of dried apples, and the purple plants also incorporate raspberry and a touch of fresh mint. This strain is suitable for regular medical use and shows it greatest applications for anxiety reduction and anti-depressive effects.

Mekong High
Dutch Passion

 75/25

 soaring, intoxicating

 fresh, earthy floral

 56–63 days

 undisclosed Vietnamese/Laotian strains

 150–350g per m² in 250–350g per plant out

 in/greenhouse preferred

Mekong High is a soaring retro sativa high that captures the glory of sativas of old. This strain is unique to a remote and largely inaccessible valley around the Vietnam/Laos border where it was highly prized by local tribesmen. Accessing this region was only possible with plenty of mountain climbing equipment and local good will. As with all Dutch Passion strains, this variety went through rigorous quality control testing before being released in order to ensure that potency and growth were fully characterized and stabilized.

Mekong High branches like a bush, so each plant needs room to form side branches in order to realize its potential. This plant forms an impressive central bud that can grow to be the length of one's arm, but it still invests a significant amount of its flowering strength in the side branches, which are nearly as long. With plenty of nutrients, Mekong high can grow to final sizes of about 6 feet (2 meters) high and nearly as wide.

When lit properly and allowed to grow to its potential, these plants yield a surprisingly generous harvest for a sativa. The industrious side branching combine with the 15 to 20 inch (40–50cm) long buds that bulk up the yield to a range more typically expected from the indica side of the family.

The Mekong High plant has many telltale characteristics that mark it as a sativa, including slender leaves that are a bright, fresh green. Late in flowering, the plants take on an exquisite, rich and spicy aroma, and some may develop copper and purple coloration on the leaves. While some sativas prove to be delicate, these plants are robust and vigorous, showing resistance to mold and bud rot.

This crop provides some enviable sativa headstash. Mekong High is an original, fresh, pure-smoking sativa that reminds people of the way sativas used to be. The harvested buds are sticky and scented with the intoxicating, spicy aroma that perfume the growroom near harvest. The taste is distinctively earthy and pleasant. The true highlight of this strain is its happy, uplifting effect. It is exceptionally clear, making it wonderful for creativity and socializing. The strain will be cherished by sativa connoisseurs!

Dutch Passion –
The Story of Mekong High

Mekong High was a labor of love. This strain was found in a very remote valley that was known by the locals for producing exceptional marijuana. Locating this strain required months of field visits to the jungle area in and around the Vietnam/Laos border, where numerous wild varieties were examined and rejected before the desired pure genetics were found. Acquiring this variety required careful diplomacy with local tribal elders to access the valley where it grows.

Local tribespeople use this strain only for special occasions. They had not traded their strain with other tribes, making Dutch Passion confident that it is an unadulterated variety new to the market. While its genetic heritage in the equatorial Mekong Delta limits its adaptability to outdoor gardens in temperate regions, this plant is hardy when grown indoors or in the greenhouse. Some European growers have reported that a single Mekong High plant is quite capable of filling an entire greenhouse.

After the trek to find this unique strain and the work to stabilize it, Dutch Passion feels the resulting Mekong High strain was well worth the effort. This variety will be a gem in the collection of any sativa connoisseur. Experienced testers likened this variety to the elite sativas circulating in Amsterdam during the 1970s and '80s, and gave it top ratings for quality.

Smoke a little on a beautiful summer's day and let yourself be transported back to simpler times and scenic places. You'll understand why this strain is more than just a tribute to the past, but also looks to the future. After being introduced in 2010, this sativa has already begun to attract interest. Expect to hear more about the pleasures of Mekong High in the coming years.

Morning Glory
Barney's Farm

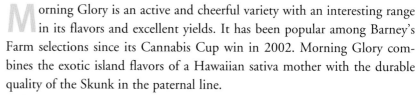

Morning Glory is an active and cheerful variety with an interesting range in its flavors and excellent yields. It has been popular among Barney's Farm selections since its Cannabis Cup win in 2002. Morning Glory combines the exotic island flavors of a Hawaiian sativa mother with the durable quality of the Skunk in the paternal line.

Skunk varieties are known as versatile plants that contribute many desirable and durable qualities to more delicate and challenging strains. Sativas are generally known to be lankier and more finicky in the garden, and this can often be a greater concern with varieties adapted to specific locales. Hawaiian varieties, like other island-acclimated strains, may lose their special Polynesian flavors and vibe when moved to more temperate locations. In Morning Glory, the Hawaiian mother has been infused with skunk genetics, adding a hardy efficiency to its growth. Yet the surprisingly subtle earthy floral flavors of the Skunk also allow the island qualities to drive the flavors and effects.

 60/40

 cheerful, thoughtful

 nutty, grapefruit, spice

 65–70 days

 ♀Hawaiian sativa x ♂Skunk II

 50–100g/plant in 200–500 g/plant out

Morning Glory plants are somewhat branchy, working best when branches are retained rather than pruned to a single-stem plant. This plant's growing structure is truly hybrid, with medium leaves and a medium growing height and structure. Barney's Farm recommends growing Morning Glory in soil with organics. Plants finish in early October outdoors, or in 8–10 weeks of flowering indoors, with average yields of 450 grams per square meter.

In their natural state, Morning Glory buds have a distinctly strong, citrus aroma, but the smoke is mild and just a bit earthy and spicy, with subtle hints of almonds and white pepper. The high is soaring yet simultaneously relaxing. It can enhance energetic or social activities, making it a true "morning glory," yet it serves equally well when more sedentary or passive activities are planned, whether laying on the beach or simply watching a summer movie.

Morning Star
Seeds of Freedom

Photos: Breeder D

Morning Star was developed in 2004 with outdoor growing in mind. The goal was to create a potent, high-resin variety that finished early. Breeder D, the chief genetic engineer at Seeds of Freedom took one of his favorite plants, an F2 Sensi Star female, and crossed it with an early flowering Leda Uno male. In testing, this male reacted quickly to the change in photoperiod. The male Leda Uno helped increase the yield and shorten the ripening time, producing plants that finish early with impressive resin development and potency.

Morning Star seeds produce fast growing seedlings that develop into sturdy, branchy plants. The plants are light green color at optimum health, producing thin, long, sativa-like leaves with a slight internode stretch. Because plants are speedy and branchy growers, they establish themselves quickly outdoors and can get quite large, especially if they were started indoors and then moved outside. Plants that are pruned can get very bushy from the strong side branching, which leads to large yields. One must take care when growing outdoors during a wet season, as some mold problems can occur. This variety has been cultivated outdoors since its creation, and the ripening time is fairly consistent and reliable. It can be harvested from September 1–15th in Ontario, which is between 42–52° North latitude.

Morning Star is low on the smell factor while in the garden, exuding a fresh aroma that makes it suitable for indoor gardens, where it is best as a multi-branch plant. If the bottom branches are trimmed, these plants can also work in a sea of green, producing large yields of fruity floral buds when flowered for 7–8 weeks. The taste has a fruity lemon-citrus subtlety, even exuding a slight citrus tone on the exhale.

Morning Star produces a cheerful, upbeat, and functional buzz, which makes it a great smoke among friends. The high comes on quickly and is fairly long lasting. This is a great smoke to start off the day. With its delightful taste and motivational high, it may just become your Morning Star.

 60/40

 cheerful, happy, social

 fruity lemon floral

 49–56 days

 ♀ Sensi Star F2 x ♂ Leda Uno

 40–50g per plant SOG ; 60–100g per plant multibranch 500g per m² out

 out preferred

Marijuana: Existential Connector
By Ed Rosenthal

The brain is a filter that has been organized by the culture it has learned. As new information enters, it is processed along the lines already developed. Most of this filtering takes place in the unconscious. It uses much more energy and performs much more signaling than the conscious. You can think of the conscious part of the brain, what we are aware of, as the tip of an iceberg.

How does sensation and thought bubble up to consciousness, anyway? That last sentence was just a random thought that bubbled up—but then everything bubbles up. Do you know what you are going to say before you say it? Or does it just flow out? Do you sometimes surprise yourself with your own thoughts or words? Did they erroneously flow through the filter

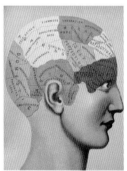

that your learning imposed on your brain's organization? In the first five years of your life, the culture you were living in shaped the organization of your brain. This is the filter through which you process the information that flows in each and every day.

Usually the brain filters out information or thoughts that don't fit into its organizational structure. Huxley mused that psychedelic substances hinder the brain's ability to filter random thoughts. When you are high, more thoughts and sensations pass through the filters so consciousness races with thoughts and new ways of sensing your surroundings. He wasn't alone in this observation. In *Botany of Desire*, Michael Pollan suggests that psychoactives such as marijuana serve as "cultural mutagens" because they change the texture of your thoughts, taking you off the beaten path that socialization has led you to habitually follow.

Soma and friends enjoying cannabis in Vondel Park, Amsterdam. *Marijuana helps people develop bonds with each other.*

The process of being high is both very intimate and very expanding. Who knows your thoughts but you? Others have only glimpses of what you think, but most of the ideas and sensations that continually float through your consciousness are internalized and can never be resolved. Describe the taste of chicken. Do we all see the same green? What does an orgasm feel like? We are together, we commune, but still each person is sort of a floating island. Only part of the consciousness is visible; the rest lies beneath the surface.

The experience itself, though trapped in our individual brains is a shared state of consciousness that binds people who participate. It is almost Gnostic; the inner circle has the secret knowledge. Everybody has his or her own version of the same event. Everyone knows it, but at the deepest level it is too personal to share. It's not that we don't try; it's just impossible to describe. Words are simply an approximation. They are just our way of making contact with a world outside of ourselves.

Music may be an even more universal way for humans to communicate. With words, you have to know the language. But sounds don't need to be translated to affect your brain, which you experience as affecting your emotions. Most people wouldn't play a march to get into a romantic mood.

MardiGrass held in Nimbin, NSW Australia, 2008. Thousands from all over the world come to celebrate the harvest every year.

Marijuana is a mild psychedelic. It opens your mind, lets it wander, and helps you get closer to your senses. Listening to music becomes enveloping. When people listen as a group they develop a bond because although each has had their own experience, they know that they have all had one.

This universality of knowing that each person in a group is having a profound individual intimate experience creates a bridge across our individual consciousnesses. It brings to mind videos of groups of squid all signaling together in the same pattern and then all changing the pattern at the same time. The squid employ synchronous patterning to bridge the space between individuals.

Marijuana bridges the gap. Everyone likes it. No matter your gender, your sexual orientation, your age, your race or ethnicity, once you share marijuana with another, you develop a tiny bond, even if for a fleeting moment—even if you never see the person again. It's not quite spiritual, but it is often meaningful. It's a reprieve from the ordinary. A time out to regroup and let the brain wander and to experience a little bit more of yourself and those around you.

Marijuana brings us together.

Photo: Jack F6, courtesy Sannie's See

Mr. Nice
Sensi Seed Bank

Mr. Nice was named in honor of Howard Marks, the Welsh cannabis campaigner, author, and one-time hashish entrepreneur. Marks became a folk legend after writing his bestselling 2002 autobiography Mr. Nice, which tells the story of his life as an international marijuana smuggler during the 1980s leading up to his DEA bust. In 2010, his story was made into a movie out of the UK, which was also titled Mr. Nice. Marks continues to write about marijuana and to advocate for its legalization.

His namesake strain also starts with weed folklore. The Mr. Nice mother is a G-13. G-13 is the rumored US government pot from their Mississippi facility. An unknown technician rescued a cutting from this facility, after which it was brought to Holland. This 100% indica strain is an Afghani genotype. The Mr. Nice father is Sensi Seed Bank's Hash Plant, a cross that is 75% Hash Plant and 25% Northern Lights.

In Mr. Nice, these two power-hitters combine to deliver a vigorous and iconic indica. Deep jade and short in stature, these plants support heavy bud production with outstanding resin levels on sturdy thick stems. Much like Mr. Nice himself, the G-13xHP seed strain was big in the 1980s, when it earned quite a reputation after its introduction. However, it was only released as a limited edition at the time and soon became a rare find. In 1999, Sensi brought this legendary cross back to honor a living legend.

Mr. Nice forms a very large central cola, and its restrained growing pattern allows it to grow admirably in a sea of green setup without being overly crowded. Growers looking for a star indica will enjoy the efficiency and vigor of these tough and capable plants in the garden. Yields are admirable, even when plants are kept small.

Indica connoisseurs will savor this variety's mouth-watering "double Afghani" bouquet. The dense bud clusters ripen into a rich, spicy-sweet tang of raw resin glands, blended with dark, earthy undertones. When sampling the stickiest nuggets, the taste can convince people that they're smoking a mix of hashish and ganja. The potency of the stone may test people's limits with its knock-down Afghani body rush.

 I

 stoney, body relaxation

 earthy, hashy

 60 days

 ♀ G-13 x ♂ Hash Plant

 up to 100g

 SOG

Northern Light x Apollo G13
Biotops/Queen Seeds

The Apollo G13 mother is a sativa from the US. Northern Light is a 50% Afghan, 50% Thai mix combining genetics from Holland and the US. In this cross Biotops/Queen Seeds made their selections in Holland to produce a versatile variety that has won awards in both indoor and outdoor cup categories in Europe.

The Northern Light x Apollo G13 grows best outdoors in Mediterranean climates where it will finish by mid-October if started in mid-July. Depending on how intense the sun or lighting is, plants that enter flowering when they are a foot tall (30–35cm) will finish between 6–9 feet (2–3 meters). This is a cooperative plant indoors, where it shows good resistance to pests and maintains satisfying yields even when conditions fluctuate. It can be grown in hydro or soil and does well in a sea of green setup because it is a compact plant. There is little branching, and the branching that it forms stays short. Because of its growth pattern, Northern Light x Apollo G13 looks like a skinny pine tree,

 60/40

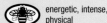 energetic, intense, physical

 citrus, spicy-sweet

 60–65 days

 ♀Apollo G13 x ♂Northern Light

 450–600g per m² in 750–1000g per plant out

 SOG

but more importantly, forms a huge central bud. Biotops recommends planting 12 plants per square meter in sea of green for yields about an ounce (25–30g) per plant. Multi-branch indoor plants may take up more space and yield an average of just under two ounces (50g) per plant. The plants have a short to medium gain in stretching size, and the smell is discreet as long as the temps don't range too high.

The Northern Light x Apollo G13 buds have a compact structure that forms pyramids of green with a lot of resin gain and hairs that darken to brown by maturity. The leaves vary from slender to a more hybrid medium, and the colors are intense to clear green depending on the fertilization routine. One trick for big yields: this variety likes its PK, so be generous. Hash fans will find this variety can make some primo hash stash.

The Northern Light x Apollo G13 strain is a no-nonsense, connoisseur strain that can be appreciated by beginners, therapeutic smokers, and seasoned tokers alike. The smell has a citric spice with a hazy edge, while more sweet and floral notes come through in the flavor. The high is clear with a fast approach. The long lasting Zen mind state extends to relaxation in the body, with therapeutic applications for muscle relaxation. If harvesting is prolonged until the 10th week, the higher CBD and CBN accumulation create a stronger sedative effect that works well for insomnia. This strain won 1st prize at the 2005 Cannabis Champions Cup in the Outdoor category and 2nd prize in the 2008 *Highlife* Cannabis Cup Barcelona in the Hydro category.

NYPD (New York Power Diesel)

Nirvana

The New York Power Diesel (NYPD) is an indoor power strain with a radical mix of Sativa Mexicana father and Afghan/Dutch indica mama. The Nirvana addition to the diesel family stays close to the New York variant. NYPD is an F1 hybrid that is balanced but sativa-dominant, with potential for gardeners and home breeders. Its mother plant, the Aurora Indica is a combination of Northern Lights and an Afghan strain that was stabilized especially for use in this cross. The heavy, greasy narcotic effects of the Aurora Indica beautifully cut the edge of the crispy, speedy Oaxacan sativa father known as Eldorado. The resulting terpenoids have a powerful diesel aroma with a lemon-edged fuel flavor.

NYPD grows tall because the sativa influence creates moderate spacing in the internodes and long stems. The branches are lanky but sturdy and are neither spare nor profuse, allowing the grower to decide which direction to take the gardening setup. Soil and organics maximize the aromas, but these plants are pretty dank and smelly in the grow space regardless. The dark green calyxes form chains of big popcorn buds that are surprisingly tight in structure. Hairs turn red toward maturity. NYPD yields are good—in a sea of green with 600-watt lights, gardeners can expect between 350 and 450 grams per square meter.

The New York Power Diesel is a blissful, balanced, and relaxing buzz that makes great campfire joints. It is a treat to smoke, starting with a clear, enjoyable transition and bringing a mixture of earthiness and lemon zing, over a recognizable deep note of diesel acridity. This buzz brings out a sense of calm, wonder, and sensory awareness. It can enhance discernment and pleasures. NYPD makes one notice the subtle flavors of foods, the enjoyment of the smells, sights, and sounds of the outdoors, and has potential as an aphrodisiac.

 70/30

 soaring, clear, relaxing

 lemon & earthy fuel

 65 days

 ♀Aurora Indica x ♂Eldorado

 350–450g per m²

 SOG

Oregon Pinot Noir
Stoney Girl Gardens

This variety was bred among the grapes of one of the most respected Pinot Noir vineyards in Oregon. It gets its name from where it was bred as well as the purple color of its stems and buds and the sophisticated grape aspect of its flavor. Vine-like and tropical, this plant is well suited for outdoor grows in the Pacific Northwest or similar climates—that is, moderate with plenty of rain.

Indoors, the Oregon Pinot Noir is amazingly versatile. The mother is a Purple Kush, a pure sativa from the Hawaiian Islands. This mother was truly a traditional girl, bred from 1972 Panama Red and Columbian Gold parents. She was brought from Hawaii to Oregon and then crossed with Stoney Girl Gardens' Pit Bull. The Pit Bull genetics reduced time to harvest and also helped the plant acclimate to its cooler home off the island. As a result, this durable cross can finish in a quick 6 weeks of blooming, remarkably fast for a strain that is sativa-dominant in effects.

Pinot Noir grows long and lanky, reaching 6–7 feet at finish. Outdoors, this plant has been grown as tall as 15 feet, with per-plant yields averaging in multiple pounds. The growth pattern of the Pinot Noir is more like a spider plant than a typical tree structure, getting wider than it is tall and forming bottom branches very low on the plant. Its abundant arms form many colas with close nodes. As such, Pinot Noir is best as a multi-branch plant in soil and works well in a screen of green setup. Because of its bendable, vinelike branching, this strain can be trained to a lattice or grown as a low-profile plant that blends with the surrounding scenery. It is also ideal for raised beds or container gardening. In most indoor growing scenarios, it doesn't hurt to stake this plant's pliable branches to create a more orderly canopy, but the branches are sturdy enough to stand on their own.

Gardeners who take pleasure in color variation will enjoy this plant's purple tones. The stems tint to a faint purple that deepens as the plant ages. The bright tones of the thin sativa leaves fade to purple. The Pinot buds are bright and long, with wispy-haired pistils that are typical of Hawaiian strains. They start as little white fluffs that develop into dense, purple golf balls forming chains up the stem. Plants can easily produce 4–5 ounces per plant in an indoor grow with good methods.

Oregon Pinot Noir tastes like sweet grape with an edge of haze. It has retained delicious tropical qualities, adding notes of melon, nuts, candy, and earthy honey. Although sativa-dominant, this strain has a noticeable body effect, which can enhance pleasures and even serve as an aphrodisiac, but may trigger couchlock or cause mental wandering at larger doses. Overall it is a lingering mellow eyedroop high best saved for an evening smoke since its stonier, sleepier side may turn wake-and-bake into nap-time or interfere with the day's motivations.

  80/20

 body relaxing, eyedroop, dreamy, creeper

 candy grape with a hint of haze

 38–45 days

 ♀ Hawaiian Purple Kush x ♂ Pit Bull

 200g per plant in 1000g per plant out

 out preferred

About the Oregon Pinot Noir

The thing that really stood out about this variety was the incredibly wide space that it takes up. Even the males are huge sprawling monsters with multiple colas of flowers. Oregon Pinot Noir was key in a breeding project we did for one of our testers in Southern Oregon, who requested a custom project for his vineyard garden. He had a red haired strain called "Scarlet," and he wanted something special done with her. Crossing Oregon Pinot Noir on her made for a huge sprawling bush that we called "Crimson" with that grape flavor so appropriate for the vineyard. This sativa-dominant strain performs well indoors and out in soil. The P1 parents and original genetics work was done outdoors in a vineyard alongside award-winning Pinot Noir grapes. The flavor matches the purple with tropical grape color and flavor. We recommend organics in soil for the most pleasing results.

Pit Bull
Stoney Girl Gardens

The indica-dominant Pit Bull strain begins with a trade: some P-91 seed from the university professor who created the P-91 strain. Stoney Girl was told that this strain was the government's latest G-13. P-91 came from a program at a university in Southern California that supposedly did not exist. This grandfather of the Pit Bull's paternal side was crossed with Stoney Girl's own Berkeley Blues to become a strain called Sugar Plum. Sugar Plum, an award winner that placed first in the 2003 Oregon medical cannabis awards, is Pit Bull's father. The Pit Bull mother, simply referred to as P-91, is a cross from Southern California, consisting of a G-13 mother crossed with Bull Rider.

As the name suggests, Pit Bull is a rugged, tenacious strain. The plants are vibrant, vigorous, and mite resistant. Don't mistake this stubborn determination for rigidity. Pit Bull is very pliable and obedient. She performs well in any environment and has great yields in any arrangement from a hydro closet to an outdoor farm. The Pit Bull plant is branchy with close nodes. When allowed to grow free, she forms a giant spherical bush that blooms with buds on every branch. A quick plant, she finishes flowering in an average of 6 weeks or mid-September outdoors when planted in June, even in the temperate climes of the Pacific Northwest. It is a bush indoors and a giant tower out.

During flowering, Pit Bull jumps right into action, forming open blooms covered in crystals during the first 2 weeks. The buds are large thick spheres covered in pom-pom hairs and oozing crystals. Buds have a medium density that is neither airy nor popcorn textured, but also not rock hard. The Pit Bull sugar leaves have so much crystal on them that they tend to curl. The fan leaves are large and wide and look like maple leaves. Pit Bull stays bright green unless it gets chilly in the garden—then she turns purple. The bases of the leaves are a passion purple. The branches are bright green with violet stripes highlighting the ribs.

The Pit Bull's hardiness and instinct for survival make it an ideal strain for the beginner, but the qualities will satisfy more elite tastes and impress on special occasions. The buzz is a heavy hitter that won't be a top choice for the occasional recreational user, but is well suited to medicinal use or for experienced tokers. There is a body blissfulness and a heady intense mental component that can feel a bit like a gong has been rung inside the brain. Pit Bull is thoughtful and trippy, if a bit distracted at its height. The taste and smell profiles are complex and maintain flavors throughout, including a fresh grapefruit citrus with honey, hash, and a pungent sweet tropical bass.

 80/20

 psychedelic, thoughtful, blissful

 grapefruit/melon, honey hash

 30–40 days

 ♀ Sugar Plum x ♂ pure indica

 100g per plant in 2250g per plant out

The Pit Bull Story

Pashmina, as it is known by the Hindu Monks of Varanasi, grows on the banks of the Ganges River alongside the traditional thousand-year-old varieties. The American Pit Bull variety has been spotted in cannabis hotspots in Asia and around the globe, from Japan and China, to Hawaii, Amsterdam and the West Coast of the US. This American Pit Bull is making a good will ambassador tour around the world.

Pit Bulls have a sketchy reputation for being aggressive, and we have to admit, this gal proves to be a little aggressive right off the bat. She begins bushing and throwing leaves in the first two weeks of life. This strain is a hearty, all-purpose, fast and furious producer. There is no reason to shape or top the plant as it has perfect form every time.

The Pit Bull was first introduced in late 2005 to local clinics in Oregon. She was bred to be a true medical strain. Pit Bull was created from a cross between the award winning Sugar Plum and the P-91. To create the Pit Bull, it took hundreds of F1 seeds grown through the entire life cycle of the plant. Each plant is grown to maturity and graded throughout. Extensive notes are kept including growth cycles, smell, taste, resistance, ease of reproduction and maintenance, and of course, results of the final product. Results are tallied and put before the committee for selection. The winning F1 is then bred back for the stabilization. Only the best growing, best tasting variety is stabilized to ensure that each seed will produce the same results. All our seeds are produced from the original plants and genetics, not reproductions.

The high is instantaneous and euphoric, with a wide range of medical values, including pain relief, migraines, and much more. Forget using the grinder, this stuff is way too sticky to handle like that. In lab tests we have seen a 36% THC content. Stupefying from the first hit, this strain never makes you wonder when it will start working. Pit Bull lasts a minimum of 4 hours strong, even after eating, showering or swimming. The effects are potent, fully euphoric and excellently medicinal; however, it is better for the experienced. This is not the smoke for the recreational every-so-often smoker, or for the lightweight. Even regular users should not plan to drive or otherwise do activities that could be harmful without full attention!

Pit Bull has become a popular medical strain in the Pacific Northwest for its wide range of soothing treatment for many conditions. It is listed as a neuropathic pain and depression medication by the Oregon Green Free (www.budbook.org). In testimonies, patients have explained a use of Pit Bull to wean themselves from strong pharmaceuticals.

Although each of Stoney Girl Garden's breeds differs from one another, this one really stands out as the most unique in its flavor profile. From the beginning the plant emits a strong odor of Pit—neither armpit, or wet-dog smell, but we are talking about the exotic, deep rich, unique, tropical, distinctive, fruity, skunky, complex and intense smell of some dank weed. The taste is as a good at the end of the joint as it was the first hit.

For more on Stoney Girl Gardens, see www.gro4me.com.

PolarLight
Dutch Passion

PolarLight is part of the new generation of cannabis seed technology called 'autofem' seeds. As a feminized, autoflowering plant, PolarLight allows plants to be grown from seed to finish in 8–10 weeks, with no worries about sexing or lighting adjustments.

This variety is the result of a complicated hybridization between a fast maturing ruderalis and Dutch Passion's acclaimed Isis. Isis is generally regarded as a fine connoisseur sativa with clear, energetic qualities and satisfying yields. This combination provides a fast growing, low maintenance strain that delivers potent sativa stash.

The PolarLight plant is stocky yet narrow, taking an attractive shape and forming ample, resinous buds. These plants are not overly branchy, making them suitable to the sea of green style. No matter how short the summer, outdoor gardeners should be able to target a few months of good weather to grow an ounce or two of excellent quality marijuana from each PolarLight plant they sow. In short-summer regions, seeds should be planted at the start of the warmest, sunniest part of the season, and Mother Nature will take care of the rest. Indoors, a 20 on/4 off light cycle is recommended. After about 2.5 weeks of vegetative growth, PolarLight automatically transitions into the flowering stage for about 7 weeks. At finish the average height is around 2 feet (50–70cm). While the per-plant yields of 25–50 grams are modest, this is offset by the fact that it is possible to complete two or three separate crops in a year. These plants can be grown in pots or directly in the ground.

Autofem seeds are making headlines for all the right reasons. Their ease of growth, short season, and highly adaptable nature make them a fast track plant for quality stash. Growers who like to work with autofem seeds are encouraged to try this strain and prepare to be dazzled by the twinkly, attractive buds that result.

PolarLight's colas are not only solid, compact, and resinous, but their aroma has delicious notes of the fruity-sweet and some spice with hints of haze. The genetic heritage from the Isis gives a great sativa stone that will appeal to haze enthusiasts. This is a clear, cerebral, and energetic high, a lasting experience that may seem to soar ever higher over its duration. PolarLight is a good strain to get the creative juices flowing.

 clear, energetic

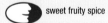 sweet fruity spice

 45–55 days

 Isis x ruderalis

 25–50g per plant

Purple Voodoo
California Bean Bank

In the Purple Voodoo strain, voodoo is used to describe the magical transformation this plant undergoes during flowering. The actual word "voodoo" comes from the word for spirit in the language of the West African country once called Dahomey and now known as the Republic of Benin. The voodoo religion acknowledges only one God, but does not think that God intervenes in human affairs. Instead, intercession in daily life is left to the spirits, who preside over minor matters and smooth the way for their followers. In this light, Purple Voodoo might be thought of as a manifestation of the purple spirit of cannabis. Certainly the genetics are purple on all branches of this California strain's family tree. The mother is Double Purple Doja, a cross of Apollo 13 and Black Russian that stays short and thick, and gains dark rich burgundy tones at finish. The father is a cross of the deep purple Urkel and Purple Diesel strains. This dad strain was chosen because it adds excellent node stacking and produces heavy buds.

Purple Voodoo is a great outdoor strain in California or similar climates such as parts of Spain. Gardeners will have to make adjustments for higher elevations or particularly humid regions to ward off mold from the sizeable buds. They finish in mid- to late October, reaching maximum heights of 6 feet (2 meters) when they are not topped. Even when grown indoors, this strain fares best when allowed to flower from multiple branches. It has amazing results when topped early and allowed to develop massive upper buds. Growth in this variety is very homogenous, with plants forming sturdy, orderly branches and maintaining an even canopy. Indoor plants double in height during flowering, finishing around 4 feet (120cm). When a sea of green technique is used, plants can be forced when they have 8 true leaves, and finish between 2–3 feet (80–100cm).

Purple Voodoo's vegetative cycle proceeds in normal fashion. The plants develop large, long branching and stack internodes well. Then, a few weeks into flowering, the magic show begins. Dark purples, yellows, oranges and bright vibrant greens start to transform the plants into technicolor beauties. The Purple Voodoo buds start as pompoms, and then spread along the branches, consuming them in a large cola casing. By week five, trichome production picks up and a dank yet floral fragrance begins to permeate the garden. Then the purple genetics kick in, transforming the buds into massive vibrant Voodoo colas that range in tone from a dark purple-black to an electric bright violet.

The Purple Voodoo smoke is smooth and flavorful with a savory edge and a pungent odor. The effect is like a potent spell that induces relaxation and a bit of trance-like stoniness lingers. It is better suited for a lazy afternoon or evening rather than as a workday smoke.

relaxing, mellow

deep smooth purple

55–65 days

♀ Double Purple Doja x Urkel x ♂ Purple Diesel

120g per plant in
150g per plant out

SOG

Qleaner
TGA Seeds

 60/40

 fast, cerebral, zingy

 candy grape

 56–63 days

 ♀Jack's Cleaner x Purple Urkle x ♂Space Queen

 450g per m²

Qleaner's true beginnings are with its Jack's Cleaner mother. Jack's Cleaner is a complex cross, which began by pairing Pluton and Neville's 1985 Super Sativa Seed Club (SSSC) Northern Lights#5. Through multiple steps, Purple Haze and Jack Herer were also introduced to the Jack's Cleaner genetic mix. The name Qleaner reflects the strong influence of Jack's Cleaner in its flavor and effects, but the Q comes from the influence of the father, a west coast mix of Purple Urkle and Space Queen.

Due to her short frame, Qleaner performs well indoors, producing good yields in both soil and hydroponic set ups. When hydro methods are used, this strain tends to experience a fast growth spurt. In soil, Qleaner plants should be topped and trained to maximize light, which greatly improves garden yields. Short vegetative times in hydro will deliver yields of about 2 ounces per site. In soil, 5 ounces per plant is average. Plants budded at 24 inches finish at a height of less than 5 feet. Topped Qleaner plants get very wide and have a great deal of lower branching. This plant forms enormous fan leaves, which should be removed from the lower branches lest they serve as umbrellas shading light from peripheral bud sites. When left untopped, the lower branches shoot up until they are almost equal in height with the top cola.

Outdoors, Qleaner's growth takes off fast. She looks like a different plant when compared to her indoor cousins. At 42° North latitude, Qleaner finishes by mid to late October. Longer grow seasons would allow the plants to have extended flowering time and grow larger.

The Qleaner has a thick musty grape scent while growing but tends to keep its smells trapped unless a flower is manipulated. As the plants progress, the leaves get an oily, leathery look and take on purple tones when the nighttime temperatures dip. The buds fill out nicely as plants near ripeness, and the leaves turn so deeply purple that they appear nearly black by harvest time. Qleaner buds are dense and crunchy to the touch due to the thick layer of encrusted bulbous trichomes. When trimming, black resin builds up on scissors and must be tasted to believe the strong grape experience.

The first thing you notice with the Qleaner is the strong candy grape flavor. Clone selection was guided by flavor, and the unmistakable tastes of grape Kool-Aid dominate, with floral fruity hints adding dimension. Almost a stimulant at the outset, Qleaner comes on very fast with an initial clearheaded, clean feeling buzz. For the first half hour, the high continues to build until it starts moving down into the body. As such, this variety is an exhilarating experience, adding a general sense of giddiness to the atmosphere, but as the full potency kicks in, watching TV may be about all you can handle. Getting a light buzz may create an electric energy, but overconsumption often leads to a strong tendency to couchlock. Subcool recommends this variety for tinctures, which provide very good pain relief when applied both externally and internally. Hints of grape flavor carry through when glycerin is used as the base.

Querkle
TGA Seeds

Photo: Subcool: Plants in photos were grown by Dioxide

The name "Querkle" is a clever twist on this indica-dominant strain's heritage. The mother strain is the Purple Urkle, a memorable Pacific Northwest variety that is easily recognized for her super short stature, slow growth pattern, and amazing transformation in late flowering to a lavender goddess reeking of grapes and purple goodness. In a linguistic mash up of the parentage, Querkle takes its "Q" from the male Space Queen used in this breeding line. Space Queen is one of Subcool's breeding projects that combines the well-known BC strain, Romulan, and the famed Cindy99 from the Brothers Grimm. The breeding male of Space Queen, nicknamed "Space Dude," is good for adding speed and stretch to most crosses.

Querkle has wide leathery leaves and a typical short, thick indica profile. It thrives indoors or outdoors in climates that have good weather until late October. These moderate feeding plants have almost no stretch, so they can be vegetated longer in order to gain size. Even though they stay compact, Querkle's internodes are tight. Breeder Subcool recommends topping them early. It is also a good idea to thin out the fat lower fan leaves to allow light to reach the lower branches. Once topped, Querkle plants form large three-headed bushes with bottom stems as big around as your thumb. When given sufficient vegetative time, topped, and grown in soil, plants consistently yield 4 ounces each.

A sea of green method can also be used. Clones that are budded at 12 inches (30cm) produce about ¾ ounce (21g) per bud site. These plants also do very well when untopped and grown in a screen of green style. Beginners and advanced growers all seem to enjoy growing Querkle. Fans of color will be thrilled by this plant's transformation as it flowers. The undersides of the fan leaves turn the rich reds of burgundy wine midway through flowering. As they reach maturity, the leaves and stems become dark purple, and the entire plant takes on a purplish-silvery black shading. Buds are dense and heavy with a purple tint.

Querkle is mostly a nightcap smoke, and may encourage late night snacking. It can also be a nice companion for hikes or other mellow outdoor activities. The buzz comes on slowly and lasts a long time. The sensational flavors are worth cleaning out the pipe or bong so they can be thoroughly savored. This strain's primo taste and the gradual buzz may take discipline to avoid the heavy zoned stone of overindulgence. Querkle is also a good choice for making tinctures, which are calming and very helpful with sleep disorders or nighttime leg pain.

 relaxing, mellow

 deep smooth purple

 55–65 days

 ♀ Double Purple Doja x Urkel x ♂ Purple Diesel

 120g per plant in 150g per plant out

 SOG

Subcool's Querkle Journey
Subcool
TGA Seeds

By now, many cannabis fans know of my work with Black Russian and Sputnik. Many people swear by these strains for potency and yields. There are no complaints about their flavors either, but they are often described as "berry pepper" or "spicy" and that was not the flavor profile I was looking for when I started out.

Many people go crazy for Blueberry, but in my experience, the genuinely yummy berry female is a rare find. I have wasted many a dollar in the US and in the UK as well as in Canada searching for a blue-purple plant with an outstanding flavor profile. Along the way, I've spoken with several people who grew out the purple cutting known as Urkle. This female is easily recognized by her super short, slow growth pattern and her sudden metamorphosis into a lavender beauty that is saturated with the sugary odor of grapes.

My friend Sticky Lungs passed along a cutting of an Urkle strain for me to grow out. I first enjoyed this particular Urkle specimen when Sticky himself grew out a sample, and I must say it was among the best tasting cannabis I'd had all year. For a young dude, Sticky shows an amazing understanding of the plant and his relationship with its dankness.

The cutting from Sticky took so long to get going that I moved her to the rear of the garden and lowered my expectations. Through most of the growing cycle, this plant seemed sluggish. Then like a procrastinator at the eleventh hour, this plant filled out in the last two weeks with massive rock hard colas that faded into purple. I was doubly surprised. First the growth accelerated so much it seemed like you could pull up a chair and actually watch it grow. Second, I had intentionally set conditions to inhibit purpling from any environmental source. I didn't let the night temperatures drop and I kept the plant in a slightly warmer area of the garden. I kept the nitrogen levels super high to make sure that she would stay green to the end. The only way this girl was changing colors was from naturally occurring genetic traits, but by the end she was deep purple nevertheless. The finished buds were a dark, almost black, plum color, and the flavor was out of this world. The buzz wasn't wimpy either. The heavy indica influence made it great for nighttime and was a terrific accompaniment to a nice strong sweet cup of coffee.

If Urkle had a downside, it was the length of time she took to grow after rooting. She definitely starts out as a slow-growing gal. When gardening in soil, I still take cuts of Urkle a full month before the rest of my strains just so she can have a chance of keeping up. We at TGA liked this plant a lot. After growing it out for almost a year we introduced her to our resin-making male version of Space Queen, "Space Dude." Space Dude is good for adding some speed and stretch to most of his sibling crosses, and we hoped that the combination of potency and heavy resins would make a killer cross. Urkle-Space Dude hybrids were grown out in four separate test grows to determine the consistency of coloring, and we were very happy to achieve the deep purple in high numbers. Querkle, the result of this cross, has a speedier vegetation than Urkle, although it is still slower than the average plant at the start. This variety has retained the remarkable fruity purple flavors and the strong resounding stone of its special mama plant to finally deliver the flavor profile that I was seeking in a purple plant.

Raspberry Cough
Nirvana

Raspberry Cough is a red-haired F1 cross of Nirvana's famed ICE with a Cambodian landrace mother strain. The tropical high-THC mother has characteristics similar to Thai and other regional strains from Southeast Asia that make them such enviable building blocks for excellent sativa quality. The ICE father is a red skunk with some white strains in the family tree and is a rapid growth hybrid known for above-average yields.

This hybrid is sativa-dominant, retaining some of the stretchy open structure of its mother, but she grows and finishes more quickly than pure sativa strains. Those who live in a forgiving climate can plant Raspberry Cough outside in May and harvest at the end of October. Two-thirds of the height gain happens during flowering, so indoor gardeners should force flowering with this in mind. Raspberry Cough is not too branchy and stays narrow, allowing plants to be placed close in a sea of green, with average yields in this setup between 400 and 500 grams per square meter. Like most sativa-dominant plants, Raspberry Cough's performance is very closely tied to environmental conditions.

Raspberry buds are neither fluffy nor super dense. They are thin and long, like cattails, with many red hairs. They will turn bluish if night temperatures cool down during the final weeks of flowering. The high from these frosty colas is awake yet tranquil, with a lung expansive quality. Its clearheaded, alert, and functional yet peaceful influence is recommended for medicinal purposes. It is also good for preventive medicine, rejuvenating the spirit and serving as a great companion for healthy activities such as nature hikes, meditation, or savoring the natural flavors of nature's best foods. Raspberry Cough's profusion of herb, mint, spice, and tropical floral freshness might be counted among nature's yummy offerings.

 70/30

 functional, uplifting yet calm

 fresh spicy tropical

 65 days

 ♀ Cambodian x ♂ ICE

 400–500g per m²

 SOG

The History of Cannabis Action Network and Berkeley Patients Group

By S. Newhart

Debby, Jeff Jones, and John Gilmore circa 2000

The renaissance of the grass roots movement for cannabis began in the early 1990s with the "Planting Seeds" campaign. This tour traveled across the US, holding 150 smoking events and informational rallies a year. It brought together many of the leading activists.

Fifteen core organizers served as the engine of this tour, including figures such as the Berkeley Patients Group founder Debby Goldsberry, hemp activist Jack Herer, and federal medical marijuana patient Elvy Musikka. The theme of the message they spread was threefold: personal civil liberties, marijuana's medical benefits, and the wide-ranging applications for the hemp plant.

"You couldn't go to the library to find this out—there was no information on hemp or medical cannabis there. You couldn't ask your parents, and your friends didn't know. It was something that people could not go out and find. So we had to bring the idea to the people," Goldsberry says of the tour. "They could turn on to the idea like we were turned on." And they did.

When the tour started in the early 1990s, profiling was still

Debby and Elvy

legal grounds for stopping a vehicle. The van in which they toured was regularly targeted for searches. There were almost no hemp products on the market. Police came to the rallies or events telling speakers that it was illegal for them to talk about marijuana and its uses, and generally harassing people.

"And here was this group of 18-20 year olds standing up against police who are saying 'you can't talk about that,'" Goldsberry says. The tour not only spread information, but also worked to find and assist local organizers to keep the community active on marijuana issues. "There are so many creative people in the movement. And the more people I talked to—it was epiphanies, you could see it happen right before your eyes. It was like a snowball. I don't know when the 100th monkey was . . . but the tour was creating a movement."

In any political cause, gathering and uniting people toward a common goal is necessary. But cannabis is also innately social, and this empowers the cannabis community beyond simple politics. It brings people together from all walks of life, each with their own personal story to share, unifying them in their appreciation of the cannabis plant and their belief that this plant should be legal.

When asked why this issue became so important in her life, Goldsberry simply says, "Because of the benefit of cannabis to my life. Before I was deadly shy, I couldn't even talk. Cannabis opened the world to me.

It changed my life. It was not only cannabis, but the cannabis community. It's a great group of people—open minded, creative, and because it is a group forced underground with great threat to personal freedom, there is a certain camaraderie. It attracted me instantly."

After 5 years of near-constant touring, the group took the suggestion of long-time drug policy activist Kevin Zeese and formed an organization, which they named the Cannabis Action Network or CAN. CAN briefly settled at a hemp farm in Kentucky, but later moved headquarters to Berkeley, California, where they had more practical resources at their disposal. Debby was among the founders and moved to California with the organization.

CAN's first order of business was implementing a little-known Berkeley law passed in 1979 to make cannabis legal. CAN was also active in the 1996 campaign for Proposition 215, registering 1,500 voters and coordinating statewide with the "Get out the Vote" program. When the ballots were counted, Berkeley had the highest approval for 215 in the Bay Area, with 86% in favor of medical cannabis.

CAN pursued a personal cannabis use campaign and started a group called the Berkeley Cannabis Consumers Union. They opened a local Dutch-style coffeeshop for one day each week. It lasted for 9 months, and then it was busted on a falsified search warrant.

"We fought the charges and were successful—they were dropped. Then we sued the city over it and won a settlement," Goldsberry says. But the union remained closed.

The Cannabis Action Network unites over 250 groups from all 50 states and around the world in a grassroots coalition. The national headquarters in Berkeley holds regular meetings and serves as an information clearinghouse and support center for activist campaigns.

"At that point, some medical marijuana users came and said that they'd joined the BCCU because they needed other services too," relates Goldsberry. The Berkeley Patients Group (BPG) was formed. This center continues to operate as a health center for its patient members. In addition to creating access to safe medical-grade cannabis for its patients, BPG offers a community with alternative health resources and activities. Yoga, acupuncture and massage are among the services provided to members.

Local cooperatives formed an overarching organization called

Ed Rosenthal speaking at a CAN rally, 2001

the Alliance of Berkeley Patients, which maintains operational and healthcare standards throughout the city's cooperatives. Berkeley has worked with the clubs, approving their system of self-regulation.

Having celebrated its 10th anniversary in 2009, the Berkeley Patients Group is one of California's oldest and most respected medical cannabis collectives. The patient collective model brings together medical users in a community. It allows people to enjoy activities together and get accurate information about everything from the laws to cultivation.

Skunk Haze

Coffeeshop Classics by Ceres Seeds

 55/45

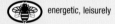 energetic, leisurely

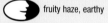 fruity haze, earthy

 70 days

 ♀Haze x ♂Skunk #1

 1g per watt

The Skunk Haze is a straightforward combo of two classic strains, each with their own strong fan base. The Haze has become a widely used addition to hybrids because people appreciate its unique soaring, lucid, happy high, but gardeners also know that this plant unhybridized is a sprawling and finicky lady to grow. The Skunk #1 is a well established, solid plant whose agreeable cultivation qualities and flavorful yields deliver a pleasant, balanced high. For this reason, Skunk #1 has been a great equalizer in breeding, a natural choice to serve as a palette on which to paint more exotic flavors and effects while sneaking in the Skunk's more reliable growth characteristics.

This addition to the Coffeeshop Classics line is truly a hybrid of its parents. It has retained the lanky, willowing branches of the Haze. At maturity, the buds make the branches top heavy and are best supported by netting or in a screen of green garden. The Skunk's influence diminishes the stretchiness, reduces the time spent in flowering, and creates a denser cola, leading to a more manageable beginner-friendly plant.

At finish, Skunk Haze is taller than the average hybrid, a happy medium between the typical Skunk and the typical Haze. The open structure is a swooping inverted triangle with light, fresh green tones and slender sativa leaflets. The buds stay pale green and form orange hairs. Because the Skunk Haze balances indica and sativa qualities, the buds aren't too compact and resist mold well. In fact, this plant likes a moist environment and thrives in a garden that mimics the tropics in heat and humidity. Keeping the humidity low will bring out more of the skunk qualities. Outside of equatorial locales, this variety makes a better indoor grow. The open structured qualities of the Skunk Haze also make it a whole lot smellier than the typical indica or hybrid.

Beginning cultivators with a yen for haze, or a general sativa-leaning will be satisfied with this variety. While growing, the haze smell is dominant, but when breaking buds, the Skunk's florid tones will be evident. Both are truly carried through in the flavor, which tickles the nose with fruity haze, but leaves an undertone of musk and earth from the Skunk lingering on the palate.

The Skunk Haze is primarily a head buzz with a lingering body stone that carries through. When plants are harvested after two months of flowering, the cannabinoid/THC balance tends to deliver a more mental high and fluffier buds. At 70 days, the buds become denser, and the increased CBD creates a stonier effect reminiscent of Jack Flash. It is always possible to progressively harvest in order to find the best balance. Overall, this variety has an energetic and clear headed yet leisurely effect that is anxiety-reducing and low on paranoia.

Sleestack
DNA Genetics

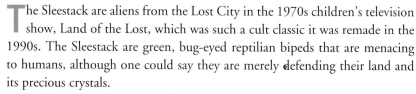

The Sleestack are aliens from the Lost City in the 1970s children's television show, Land of the Lost, which was such a cult classic it was remade in the 1990s. The Sleestack are green, bug-eyed reptilian bipeds that are menacing to humans, although one could say they are merely defending their land and its precious crystals.

The Sleestack strain may not be menacing, but she definitely contains some alien DNA. The mother is Shrom, a cross of a Colombian landrace strain called Santa Marta Gold and a Romulan indica. DNA got Shrom as a cutting from Northern California years ago. The Shrom has a satisfying yield and also a fuel haze taste that many cannabis users appreciate. Shrom is also a star when it comes to hash or concentrates, creating some clearheaded and flavorful concoctions. Sleestack's father is the Martian Mean Green a cross of Sharksbreath and G-13 Haze with an indica growth profile and deep haze aromas. Martian Mean Green crosses well as a male and imparts some of those special haze qualities without the lanky haze structure.

Sleestack is bushy with branches. She does not grow tall like the Shrom mother and also doesn't take as long as Shrom to finish. These short stout plants pack on weight after the fifth week, increasing by about 2 1/2 times the size they were at forcing by the end of 9 weeks of flowering. The plants are averse to extreme heat and will space a lot if the beginning phases of growth or flowering are too hot. However, beyond the heat sensitivity, Sleestack is an agreeable plant that the novice can grow. She bounces back from nutrient mistakes, is not prone to mold, and has proven very resistant to powdery mildew even when surrounding strains become infested.

At maturity, Sleestack is a relatively non-smelly classically shaped plant with thick, sharply serrated leaves and frosty medium-dense nuggets that are dark under their considerable bling. For the Sleestack, it is about hoarding crystals. These buds stack crystals upon crystals, becoming gaudy with frosty resin. This strain offers an unexpected, exotic smoke with medicinal value. The fuel-haze flavors carry through, leaving a pleasant taste that lingers. The high is clear headed with a slow rising onset that can become energetic and mildly psychedelic. The secret to this plant is the dry-sift kief, which is amazing and great for concentrates, especially if the concentrate doesn't require any water processing that may dull the great flavors. Kief fans or those who make any medical products from kief such as tinctures or other concentrates should consider adding this plant to the garden. Sleestack won 3rd place in the 2009 Spannabis Champions Cup in the outdoor category.

70/30

clear, energetic, upbeat

fuel haze

60–63 days

♀ Shrom x ♂ Martian Mean Green

400–550g per m²

SOG

Smoothie
California Bean Bank

The Smoothie strain actually sounds like it is made from the kinds of things you might mix up with your yogurt in the morning for a tasty treat. The mother is Blueberry and the father is Somango, two well-known flavor-heavy strains for the taste connoisseur. The well-known purple-toned Blueberry originated in DJ Short's program and gained fame on its own as well as a favorite for hybridization. Here, a more indica-type Blueberry has been used to cross with the Soma taste sensation Somango, a reddish-hued multi-hybrid that combines Jack Herer and the Big Skunk Korean.

Both Smoothie parents are branchy plants, making this strain unquestionably a multi-branch plant. As such, Smoothie thrives in a SCROG setup but can also be trained to a multi-branch SOG. The dense growth pattern of the Smoothie means growers outside of dry regions should take measures against mites and mold formation to ensure a healthy crop. Plants bounce back well as long as the underlying cause is addressed. Smoothie is a connoisseur strain that provides the motivated novice the opportunity to produce superior medication.

Smoothie powers through the vegetative cycle and finishes fast, leaping from bonsai to mile high in a short 7–9 weeks of flowering. The size and branch structure allow the grower a lot of flexibility in training the plant. Proper pruning during flowering can save a lot of effort during the harvesting phase without compromising the yield. If topped, Smoothie plants bush out, providing the potential for larger, denser top flowers. This plant's indica-style leaves turn from luscious green to a dark bluish purple and the flowers sparkle with a frost of glands.

Given the famous flavors of its parents, it probably comes as no surprise that Smoothie has an incredible bouquet. The berry-citrus perfume makes you just want to burrow your nose in and breathe deeply. This fruity-floral aroma says top-shelf quality, plain and simple. Organics in soil really brings out the flavors best, but test samples indicated little change based on variation in nutrient regimen. The blueberry sweetness comes out in the taste of the smoke. Smoothie delivers an uplifting high that feels as good as it tastes. In addition to their flavors, the Blueberry and Somango parents have reputations for sublime highs that soothe yet stimulate thought in a soaring clarity. As suggested by its name, the Smoothie transports one with a velvet touch, uplifting to a pleasant euphoria without couchlock. Relaxation or artistic endeavors pair well with this strain, but it is less suited for cognitively demanding activities. Medicinally, Smoothie offers relief from nausea, depression, headaches, cramps, and spasticity and can increase the appetite.

 70/30

 lucid, uplifting, euphoric

 berry citrus

 50–60 days

 ♀Blueberry x ♂Somango

 60g per plant in 80g per plant out

 SOG

147

SnowStorm
Dutch Passion

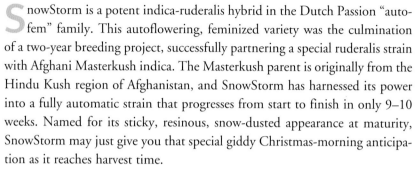

SnowStorm is a potent indica-ruderalis hybrid in the Dutch Passion "auto-fem" family. This autoflowering, feminized variety was the culmination of a two-year breeding project, successfully partnering a special ruderalis strain with Afghani Masterkush indica. The Masterkush parent is originally from the Hindu Kush region of Afghanistan, and SnowStorm has harnessed its power into a fully automatic strain that progresses from start to finish in only 9–10 weeks. Named for its sticky, resinous, snow-dusted appearance at maturity, SnowStorm may just give you that special giddy Christmas-morning anticipation as it reaches harvest time.

This variety is a strong and sturdy, low-maintenance plant that new or hobby growers will find quite manageable. Because it is feminized, no gender selection is necessary, and the autoflowering characteristic removes the need for maintaining strict light cycle phases during growth. These qualities make SnowStorm a highly adaptable choice suitable for many circumstances. Plants can be grown indoors, where they thrive under a 20-hour on/4-hour off light cycle. Outdoors, this strain only needs two months of summer weather to grow from seed to maturity. Seeds grow for 2 weeks, and then automatically switch to flowering, maturing after 7 additional weeks.

SnowStorm looks rather like a traditionally shaped Christmas tree plant, finishing at an average height of 20 inches (50cm). The leaves are of indica heritage with broad fingered leaflets. SnowStorm's buds have a semi-compact structure and exude a sticky frosting of resin that resembles a brush of winter snow. Given their modest size, these plants deliver impressive yields with a 1-ounce (25g) average and a 2-ounce (50g) maximum yield of high-quality marijuana per plant.

SnowStorm has a smooth yet sweet aroma with hints of citrus and fruit. The smoke is earthy and rich. This variety's sticky coating contributes to its potent stone, which induces a pleasant and relaxed contentedness. The indica characteristic of the high does not motivate vigorous activity, but if relaxed receptiveness is the desired mood, SnowStorm can certainly elevate the appreciation of music, art, food, and the companionship of friends.

 potent, relaxed
 earthy with a hint of fruit
 45–60 days
 Afghani Masterkush indica x ruderalis
 25–50g per plant

148

The Dutch Passion Philosophy

When we started the Dutch Passion company, we all shared a common love for the plant and an ambition to breed the best varieties. Even though our own heritage is primarily Dutch, we have worked with breeders and strains from all over the world. For us, the name "Dutch Passion" is simply the most accurate way to describe ourselves and our work.

Dutch Passion's methods tend to remain confidential as we invest heavily in pioneering breeding and genetic work. Feminized seeds and "Autofem" seeds are two examples of where we have made some unique breakthroughs. We have an ethical approach to our work. We have maintained some unique genetic lines and constantly seek out unknown genetics in the remote jungles and forests around the world where they are waiting for discovery. We genuinely don't want a single person to get into trouble by growing our seeds, so we only sell them where it is legal to do so.

Our passion for breeding and for the wonderful diversity of this plant remains at the core of our company and its work.

One of Dutch Passion's beliefs is that it is impossible to become a connoisseur of weed if you buy unknown varieties "off the street." When people grow their own weed, they can experience different types and varieties, finding the subtle differences between them. Some of our customers report that they enjoy all the varieties, but it is common for people to find one special variety that has the perfect effect for them. For example, here at Dutch Passion, one of our breeders loves the Skunk #11 while another finds the Euphoria variety to be his favorite. The strongest stone isn't always the best variety for everyone. Many people gravitate to either mainly indica or sativa varieties, while other smokers believe firmly that a strain with a balanced indica/sativa genetic heritage is best. The real question is "Which strain best suits you?" Dutch Passion's mission is to provide the answer.

Berkeley Patients Group on Dispensary Cannabis and Patient Cultivators

By Debby Goldsberry and Etienne Fontan

In state medical marijuana systems, cannabis is produced by patient cultivators or their designated caregivers and is primarily distributed collectively through non-profit dispensaries. Dispensaries are allowed to reimburse their members for the cost of producing this medicine, which has created a booming cottage industry of patient cultivators. However, very few cities and counties license and regulate cultivation, and most medical cannabis comes from small home-based growrooms. By contrast, in the Netherlands, medical cannabis is produced in 120-pound increments, and each batch can be tested one time for potency and contamination. In Berkeley, medical cannabis generally comes in one-pound increments, necessitating a complex evaluation for each unit. Further, the ban on sci-entific research and testing of cannabis products has left a vacuum of methodology. Dispensaries, in addition to serving members, have to develop reliable quality control methods on their own. BPG is leading the way on creating validated methodology for rating the potency and screening for contaminants in medical cannabis.

BPG's method of procuring cannabis for their collective members has been crafted over years of experience. Since forming in 1999, our joint experience as cannabis cultivators, clone producers, and medical cannabis patients and aficionados has shaped a successful method of determining quality and potency. Growing cannabis is easy, but consistently growing medical grade cannabis is an art. This system was developed with the help of Etienne Fontan, a combat veteran and one of the directors of Berkeley Patients Group. As a pre-215 patient, he learned to cultivate over time and has worked alongside some of the biggest names in cannabis.

BPG's policies endeavor to treat everyone with courtesy and respect. Much like other collectives, BPG only accepts medicine from members of the collective, as the law requires a closed loop of supply and distribution. When new patient cultivators arrive at BPG, they are often nervous with all of their expectations, fears, debts, and livelihood mixed into one small bag of cannabis. They are taken to a private area to discuss the medicine. BPG-trained screeners ask a variety of questions about the methods used to cultivate the cannabis, while making sure to protect the privacy of the patient cultivator. For example, they don't ask questions about the specific address of the cultivation site, the names of the cultivators involved (beyond verifying their member status), or any other question that may compromise the safety of the member. The purpose of these questions is

Headquarters of Berkeley Patients Group

Inside the dispensing room

to determine if any of the methods used for cultivation include items on the "no list" such as harmful pesticides and fertilizers.

After answering basic questions, cultivators participate in the physical inspection of their medical cannabis at a stainless steel, lab quality workstation. BPG's trained screeners use sight both magnified and not, sound, touch, smell, and taste to determine potency and to check for contaminants. They look at the overall color and size of the flower, how swollen or dense it is (given the genetics), and when it was harvested. Screeners use 30x magnification to see the size, maturity, and color of the glands on the flowers. They review the cure, flower structure, and size of the buds. Screeners also work to verify the genetics, based on their lengthy experience with the major strain types used for medical grade cannabis. They also look for abnormalities such as hermaphrodite flowers, browning, dampness, molds, mildews, bugs, excessive shake, and seeds. BPG's computer can save digital pictures

from the 30x digital magnifier, which can be used to reference the patient's harvests over time. If there are any problems, the issue is immediately shared with the cultivator.

BPG prefers to see the cannabis flowers that are about the size of an adult thumb. Large buds tend to have large stems. These stems add weight and expense to the product, and have no significant value as medicine. After receiving the marijuana, it is broken down into quality-controlled grams, eighths, and ounces for members to procure for their personal medical use. During that process, stems are removed and disposed of as waste, so too many stems can result in a medicine being turned away.

Consistently educating patients has increased the quality of the medicine BPG receives. Overall quality has improved from actively listening to what members need and then communicating these to the cannabis growers. When the medicine has passed BPG's quality control system, then the potency of the cannabis is graded based on a "star rating system." Medical cannabis flowers range in potency from high to low THC content (generally lab tested at about 3% to 26% THC). BPG rates cannabis potency for their members on ten specific scales that range from 1 to 6 stars, with some half stars in between.

BPG's screeners again use tested methods to rate potency. Visual methods determine trichome count, maturity, color, and density. This dispensary has created a time-tested method for assigning star ratings. The cannabis is rated using a nexus of quality and potency. For example, the highest rated potency with a quality below perfect would be rated 5½ stars, while pure perfection will rate a 6-star designation. In contrast, leaf product, used by members for at-home baking, is generally a 1-star designation.

Recently, BPG engaged the services of a local analytical lab to test the cannabinoid content in their medicine. After testing more than a thousand samples for cannabinoids, with THC findings ranging from 3%–25%, we have begun to compare these lab results to those determined by BPG screeners using the star rating system. Initial findings seem to show that the screeners consistently discern the accurate potency. With more research, BPG will be able to develop even more accuracy using trained evaluators. This is good news for the future, as lab testing for potency is pricey (more than $100 per sample), and like in other industries, "trained noses" are likely the most effective method to evaluate this medicine.

On average, BPG turns away 50% to 80% of the cannabis that members produce. This may be due to quality or it may be because BPG already has sufficient supply to meet patient demand. We are fortunate to have an abundance of the highest quality medicines from which to choose, and our needs change throughout the day. As we strive to fill every slot in our 6-star rating system, some days we may only need mid-grade or low-grade cannabis. Other days, we are able to procure enough of the highest-grade cannabis that BPG has to turn away even the best products.

Most patient cultivators ask what varieties BPG members wish to see. In reality, any well-grown medi-

Debby Goldsberry, founder of Cannabis Action Network and Berkeley Patients Group

cal grade cannabis is desirable. Our members suffer from many different primary medical conditions, fall into various positions on the economic scale, and like to try new strains to find new forms of relief. Mostly, what BPG members desire is a safe and pure form of medical cannabis free of contaminants with reliable and consistent potency that can be is standard across the rating system.

We would appreciate it if cultivators and cannabis geneticists would start to seriously and carefully consider the strain names they choose. While appropriate in the context of adult personal use of cannabis, many current names do not translate well into the world of medical cannabis. It is important that these medicines have names that offer hope and compassion. Naming them with disparaging or comic names, or names based on disaster scenarios miss the first opportunity to create positivity. Just like seeing someone yawn can make you yawn, seeing a positive word in a medicine's name makes people smile.

As medical cannabis becomes legal in state after state across the nation, communities must learn to effectively manage the safety issues regarding medical cannabis for their members. This will inspire future regulation and assure safety now. To help with this process, BPG co-founded, along with other collectives and stakeholders, the Medical Cannabis Safety Council (MCSC). For the last two years, BPG has sponsored scientific research and development for the MCSC. They have partnered with a talented team of researchers to develop methods to rate potency, screen for contaminants, and to develop safe handling processes that can be replicated in dispensaries throughout the country.

Berkeley Patients Group is traveling this path one step at a time. With consistent and validated scientific methods, this pioneering dispensary is helping to move the medical cannabis industry forward to self-regulation. These efforts create reasonable standards for sane and safe medical marijuana policies, with the ultimate goal of freedom for all to use this helpful medicinal herb.

Etienne Fontan (left) at the Berkeley Patients Group laboratory

Soma-licious
Soma's Sacred Seeds

This all-indica strain is not only delicious, it is Soma-licious. If you follow the breeding scene you may already know that Soma strains have a reputation as heavenly headstash that deliver on taste. Soma's reverence for the delicious is also evident in his dedication to growing with organics in soil. So when Soma says that Soma-licious is one of the tastiest strains he's ever developed, it is a safe bet to say this variety is going to deliver some fantastically dank flavors.

The Soma-licious mother is the LA Confidential developed by DNA Genetics. LA Confidential swept many awards in the mid-2000s and gathered a celebrity following. This mother plant truly captures what kush is meant to be, deriving from an OG Kush line. The stone is surprisingly energetic and super potent, closely mimicking a hash-type high. In Soma-licious, this mother has been crossed with Soma's Lavender strain, an Afghani-strong strain that combines Super Skunk, Big Skunk Korean, Afghani and Hawaiian for another strong hash-flavored contender. Lavender's name comes from the intense purple coloration this plant acquires over the course of flowering.

Soma-licious has carried the Lavender's purple genetics through, turning a vivid to dark purple over the growing cycle. This strain can be grown indoors or out, and is best as a multi-branch plant, since it stays fairly short (3 feet/1 meter) and trains fairly easily when staked or super-cropped. Outdoors, Soma-licious finishes at the beginning of October at an average height of 6 feet (2 meters).

The flavors deliver the extreme hashiness of the parents with a mixture of sweetness that pleasantly lingers on the tongue for quite some time after smoking. To maximize the chocolate earthy goodness, Soma recommends soil with organic guano as the main flowering fertilizer. However, Soma-licious delivers on more than the taste buds. The high evokes a serene yet luminous state of mind that seems to awaken a broad, almost philosophical sense of acceptance and love for what is. The stress of the modern world is swept away with this change in perspective. A little Soma-licious can make the path to kindness and patience easier to find. It is the kind of high that brings a smile and a good belly laugh. While it is terrific for enhancing enjoyment of great music, it seems to make bad music sound much worse. Those who discover this strain often seek it out. The only challenge with this strain may be making sure there's enough to last.

 physically relaxing

 earthy sweet

 70 days

 ♀ LA Confidential x ♂ Lavender

 350g per m²

Somantra
Soma's Sacred Seeds

In several Eastern spiritual traditions, mantras are special words, phrases, sounds or syllables that are chanted to manifest ultimate reality. To vocalize a mantra is to connect with the divine in a way that reaches beyond the limited understanding of the mantra's literal meaning. Somantra is a variety that embodies this heightened sense of awareness and internal transformation creating a calm sense of connection and contemplation.

This variety begins with the mother Sogouda strain. Sougouda is a mostly indica cross of Cheese, Blueberry and G-13 Haze. It is a distinctly delicious incense of pine-sandalwood mixed with the slightly floral haze and sweet smooth edge of fruit. The father is the sativa phenotype of the Kushadelic strain. Kushadelic is an OG Kush/G-13 Haze cross a slightly tangier and earthier kush version with haze highlights. Together, Sogouda and Kushadelic combine to make the largest plant in Soma's library. Somantra is an impressive plant with a tangy citrus mango flavor and a soaring meditative high.

Unless the climate is semi-tropical, Somantra is recommended as an indoor plant. When grown in the equatorial outdoors, this variety turns into a small tree by the end of the season. Even when grown indoors, Somantra is a massive plant and needs a grow space with a high ceiling. It is definitely best when allowed to form multiple branches, which are sturdy and mimic the symmetry of a candelabrum. The slender leaves reflect the strongly sativa heritage. The flowering time on Somantra is quite long, taking 3 months or more to ripen.

Finished Somantra buds are very hard and thickly carpeted with THC crystals. The hairs are prominent and stay white a long time before turning red at ripeness. The dominant flavor is reminiscent of a ripe meaty mango mixed with some good cheese. Like its namesake, Somantra awakens a sense of cosmic clarity. The effects let one soar into the wondrous mystery of existence, inspiring thoughtful time spent with friends and a great appreciation of melody and art. Fans of water hash should jump at the chance to transform their trim into some primo full melt. This strain won 1st place in the Hash Category at the 2010 Breeder's Cup in Amsterdam.

 60/40

 soaring, meditative

 mangos

 90–100 days

 ♀ Sogouda x ♂ Kushadelic (sativa pheno)

 350g per m²

 in preferred

Southern Nights
Fast Seed Bank

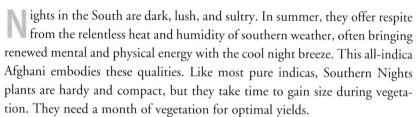

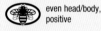
even head/body, positive

earthy, acrid, herbal

45–50 days

♀Afghani x ♂Afghani

50g in 300–400g out

Nights in the South are dark, lush, and sultry. In summer, they offer respite from the relentless heat and humidity of southern weather, often bringing renewed mental and physical energy with the cool night breeze. This all-indica Afghani embodies these qualities. Like most pure indicas, Southern Nights plants are hardy and compact, but they take time to gain size during vegetation. They need a month of vegetation for optimal yields.

When the plants have filled out, the Afghani parentage confers a fast flowering time. Southern Nights speeds through flowering in an average of 6–7 weeks. This robust plant performs well in hydro or soil, and adapts well to a sea of green setup. Outdoors, average flowering times are 45–50 days, finishing at the end of September in Mediterranean latitudes.

At the point when plants are forced to flower, it is good to trim off the lower branches and go easy on the fertilizer until they gain some size. Once growth has been established, Southern Nights resembles a compact Christmas tree with thick dark green foliage. If the leaves aren't dark and dense, the plants need more feeding. This variety is good for a beginner, but gardeners should keep a close eye on pH balance and watch for signs of nutrient buildup until they get a handle on the right fertilizer and nutrient balance. Organic fertilizers are best.

Southern Nights can handle a wide range of temperatures well. As long as the space is adequately ventilated and in a reasonable temperature range, these plants have a strong resistance to pests and do not develop a strong odor. Plants flowered at 3 feet (1 meter) finish at 4–5 feet (1.2–1.5 meters). The buds are rock hard with resinous silver-green calyxes and thick white hairs that turn coppery-brown at maturity. Yields max out at 450 grams per square meter. Clones taken from Southern Nights plants root well and fast.

The finished buds make attractive green-gray stash with an earthy green smell and flavor. The Southern Nights high is its most enviable trait—a positive mind-body effect that is great at any time of day and agrees with many types of people and personalities. It is positive and relaxing enough to be a welcome guest at the dinner party. The first thing most people notice is its fast-acting body effect. It encourages activities that stimulate the senses in a hands-on way. This may involve acting on a creative impulse, going for a hike, or indulging in other sensual appetites. When the stash is cured for 2–3 months, Southern Nights also serves as good medicine for relief from chronic pain.

Super Lemon Haze

Green House Seed Company

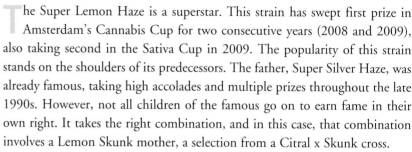

The Super Lemon Haze is a superstar. This strain has swept first prize in Amsterdam's Cannabis Cup for two consecutive years (2008 and 2009), also taking second in the Sativa Cup in 2009. The popularity of this strain stands on the shoulders of its predecessors. The father, Super Silver Haze, was already famous, taking high accolades and multiple prizes throughout the late 1990s. However, not all children of the famous go on to earn fame in their own right. It takes the right combination, and in this case, that combination involves a Lemon Skunk mother, a selection from a Citral x Skunk cross.

The Lemon Skunk mother brings a fragrant lemon intensity to tantalize haze fans, as well as adding steady skunk genetics that will appeal to growers. The haze influences still make this a better multi-branch plant. Super Lemon Haze retains a willowy sativa growth pattern and forms long buds bearded in extra long hairs. This variety does equally well in soil or hydro and prefers a high PK intake in later flowering. Although Super Lemon Haze can technically be grown both indoors and out, it is limited to the region between 40 degrees latitude North and South outdoors. It is faster and more forgiving than its haze papa, but most Super Lemon Haze growers will be gardening in the great indoors. At finish, Super Lemon Haze averages 3.5 feet indoors, but may get up to 10 feet tall in the proper outdoor setting.

The winning combination of lemon/lime pungency and strong spicy haze background is undeniably delectable. The Super Lemon Haze taste is a citrus fruity bite with a light acridity. Haze flavors of musky-woodsy earth resonate in the undertones. Flavor aside, sativa fans will really go gaga for the obvious qualities that make Hazes so well loved. The high begins with a strong and immediate physical sensation, followed by a soaring cerebral sense of elation. This pot has a fizzy social side, bringing people out of themselves into a good humored, giggly and vivacious mood. Super Lemon Haze is not for serious or heavy introspection, nor is it well suited to solitary tasks that require a single-track focus. Although it can range into the slightly dreamy, this is definitely an active, clear, and emotionally uplifting buzz that is best suited to recreational activities. Medicinally, it has been reported as good for appetite stimulation and nausea.

S I

euphoric, intense, electric

acrid fruity, musky-woodsy haze

63–70 days

Lemon Skunk x Super Silver Haze

100–200g per plant in 750–1000g per plant out

Swiss Cheese
Nirvana

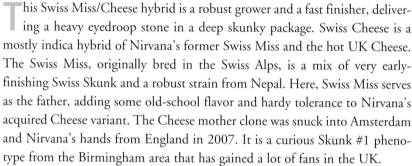

 70/30

 stoney, all-around buzz

 sweet earthy musk

 42–55 days

 ♀ Cheese clone x ♂ Swiss Miss

 400–500g per m²

 SOG

This Swiss Miss/Cheese hybrid is a robust grower and a fast finisher, delivering a heavy eyedroop stone in a deep skunky package. Swiss Cheese is a mostly indica hybrid of Nirvana's former Swiss Miss and the hot UK Cheese. The Swiss Miss, originally bred in the Swiss Alps, is a mix of very early-finishing Swiss Skunk and a robust strain from Nepal. Here, Swiss Miss serves as the father, adding some old-school flavor and hardy tolerance to Nirvana's acquired Cheese variant. The Cheese mother clone was snuck into Amsterdam and Nirvana's hands from England in 2007. It is a curious Skunk #1 phenotype from the Birmingham area that has gained a lot of fans in the UK.

Swiss Cheese is a healthy and vigorous plant that grows thick and tight with a compact take on the traditional cannabis plant structure. The leaves are thick and dark, and the buds are also a deep jade with moderate red hairs. This is a sturdy, beginner-friendly variety that is recommended for soil-based sea of green systems due to its minimal branching. The tight cola formations on these plants stink from the first flowers on. All plants appreciate perfect conditions, but Swiss Cheese is pretty flexible, handling low night temperatures without complaint, resisting mold infestations, and forgiving minor miscalculations. Swiss Cheese plants stay average in size, doubling after forcing to reach a final size of 5–6.5 feet (1.5–2 meters). They are a manageable size for smaller closet or hobby gardens. She is also fast to finish, taking only 6–7 weeks of flowering to reach maturity. The speedy cycle makes Swiss Cheese a great outdoor choice. She finishes by the beginning of September when planted in May.

Once dried, Swiss Cheese buds are dark and hard with a twist on typical skunk aromas. The mix of earthy skunk pungency with old school musk and a hint of sweet candy has an edge that makes it unique. This is a Mack truck buzz, a heavy fast-onset stone that may not be sedative, but will definitely slow things down and give smokers a stereotypical eyedroop. Most people will probably lose the urge to exert much energy after smoking this strain and be content to watch sports or movies, or engage in some other undemanding pastime, but some may be more into mellow open-ended recreation like a leisurely hike or even a jog. The body relaxation of this new 2009 strain offers an interesting flavor choice for those looking for physical relief or sedative effects.

Tahoe Gold
Master Thai Organics

 50/50

 blissful, functional, happy

 pungent tropical berry

 55–65 days

 ♀Thai/Skunk #1 x ♂Afghan/Hindu

 112–450g per plant in 1500g per plant out

 SOG

Tahoe Gold is a 50/50 sativa/indica hybrid that mixes four classic "heirloom" strains of 1970s landrace cannabis. The mother is the sativa side, a tall airy stinky-sweet bush that combines a 1975 Thai strain grown from seed with a circa 1976–1977 Skunk #1. The indica father is a cross of a 1974 Hindu Kush and a 1977 variety from Afghanistan.

This agreeable plant was bred at high altitude—just over 7,000 feet, so it fares well at low to high altitudes. Tahoe Gold grows well in any method or setup, but particularly likes coco coir and guano fertilizers. These plants spread out as they branch, but they tend to form one big fat bud on the main stem, making them suitable for a sea of green grow. Tahoe Gold plants start slowly, gaining speed as they progress, and loading on weight during the last two weeks of flowering. Plants need at least 9 weeks after flower forcing. Impatient harvesters who pluck their buds before a full 63 days will significantly decrease the yield. Outdoor flowering times are a little longer, typically about 10–11 weeks, finishing in the second half of October.

These balanced hybrids form wide pine trees with serrated medium leaves and rock hard colas. Tahoe Gold is good for both beginning growers and more experienced gardeners after a connoisseur harvest. Because these are responsive and resilient plants, they can help the beginner learn gardening basics and graduate from cannabis cultivation 101 with a completed garden of connoisseur yields. Indoor plants finish at about 6–7 feet (3 meters) and have per-plant average yields around 3.5 ounces (100g), but outdoor plants may get as tall as 10–12 feet (4 meters) and produce a whopping 4 pounds apiece (~2kg).

The Tahoe Gold variety gets its name from the attractive red-gold hues of the finished buds. These colas hearken back to the 1970s when varieties such as Panama Red or Acapulco Gold were top shelf, even though this strain's parentage derives from other geographic regions. These buds have an interesting, gilded appearance and a blissful and balanced high. Tahoe Gold invites a relaxing state of body and mind. Its functional buzz gradually takes effect, like sailing on a gentle breeze. It invites a playful and positive attitude. The smell and flavors are tropical and sweet, like a pungent berry candy. When made into hash or cooked into food, this variety can make the eyes very heavy and affect one's balance. The breeder of Tahoe Gold is a medical user with permanent nerve damage, and this is his pot of choice for pain management. Others with chronic pain conditions may also find this strain offers effective pain relief in combination with a lucid and awake state of mind and a happy attitude.

Drying and Curing Cannabis: The Art of Enhancing Effect and Flavor
By Franco
Green House Seed Company

Every cannabis gardener begins a new crop hoping to nurture healthy plants that deliver fat, tasty buds. Every crop involves months of hard work, from selecting varieties to vegetative growth, flowering, ripening, and harvesting. After all the effort, commitment, and

Freshly harvested bud with fan leaves trimmed off.

waiting, the final stage arrives. It's too late to correct mistakes made during flowering, but it is never too late to improve the flavor and the high of your buds by implementing a controlled drying and curing process.

Drying for Success

Drying is as important as growing, and a bad drying process can ruin even the best buds. Drying marijuana means reducing the water content of the buds to 10-15%, depending on the desired crispiness of the final product. Most commercial growers do not cure their crop; they just dry it and sell it. Curing is a long but necessary step toward the highest possible quality of the smoke. For the real connoisseur, curing is the essence of it all, the culminating moment towards the perfect result.

There are many ways to cure and dry, but the method I like best is to use a climate-controlled room. The room should be lit using special green fluorescents or LEDs, because the green spectrum does not affect the plant material. The temperature and the humidity must be constantly controlled and adjusted, and the air exchange needs to be calibrated exactly to the desired volume.

In an ideal situation, most of the moisture should evaporate from the bud during the first three days, and then the drying process should be slowed. To achieve this rate of evaporation in the first three days, a temperature of 68° F (20° C) and a relative humidity of 55% will ensure that the buds get to roughly 30-40% water content. From this moment on, the temperature should be dropped a few degrees down to 64° F (18° C) to slow the drying process. This allows the chlorophyll to decompose and the starches to be used up. If it dries

Manicured bud ready for drying. Photo: Subcool

too quickly more the chlorophyll will remain, and the smoke will be bitter and have a green aftertaste. The humidity of the air is also critical: If it drops below 50%, the buds will dry too fast. A timer and heater/air conditioner system with humidity control will regulate air. In total, the drying process takes around 10 to 14 days for a perfect taste.

Taste is not the only variable affected by the drying process; the high is also affected. The longer the buds are dried, the more THC will degrade into CBN and other cannabinoids. Therefore even in the same strain, the effect will slightly change from higher to more stoned, from uplifting to more physical. The difference between drying 10 days and 14 days is not very evident to the novice, but creates a world of difference to the connoisseur.

After drying, gardeners package the crop. Commercial producers usually dry the buds to 15% water content; this results in a heavier product. (More water equals more money.) Connoisseurs like to use bud that has

Buds drying on screens saves space and allows air to circulate freely.

80% water content because the flavor improves and the weed burns better. If the buds are to be smoked with tobacco, higher water content is preferable, up to 10-12% for good burning. When the weed is intended for vaporizing, it is best to leave even higher water content, 12 to 15%. This prevents easy combustion of smaller particles at vaporization temperature.

The Curing Process

After the drying is finished, the connoisseur will still dedicate a month or two to curing. Curing weed corresponds to aging a good wine. If the weed quality is average, it is not worth the effort and time necessary to cure it. On the other hand, if the buds are high grade, it is well worth waiting a little longer to get the best out of it.

I cure cannabis by packaging it in a wooden or cardboard box and pressing it slightly so that some of the trichomes break. Their oils and terpenes spread over the surface of the buds. After packaging, I leave the buds in

Buds cannot always be manicured when they are fresh. These buds are drying untrimmed, to be manicured later.

Left to Right:: Sativa, Sativa/Indica hybrid, and Indica buds ready to smoke.

an environment of 64° F (18° C), 50% relative humidity, and total darkness for a period of 1 to 2 months. Checking regularly ensures correct conditions. Make sure the humidity stays at 45-50% to prevent fungus and mold formation. If the buds smell moldy or like ammonia, the containers should be opened immediately, allowing the bud to dry in a warmer environment for a few hours before continuing the curing process. It is the result of curing undried plants.

Curing is an art and should be tried with small batches first. It increases the intensity of the flavor and will slowly but steadily lower THC in favor of CBN, which is much less potent than THC. The high of cured weed is always deeper and more introspective, often becoming a meditation and inner-vision tool. The flavor becomes much more complex and refined, gaining in depth as well as in variation of bouquet.

Cured buds that were started a little moist look slightly brownish and have a typical deep smell, one that real smokers love from the bottom of their souls. Buds cured when they were dryer retain more THC, chlorophyll, and a fresher bouquet. Like very good aged wine, there is something unique about a well-cured crop that any aspiring connoisseur should experience at least once.

For more on Franco, see
www.myspace.com/francogreenhouse

Taiga
Dutch Passion

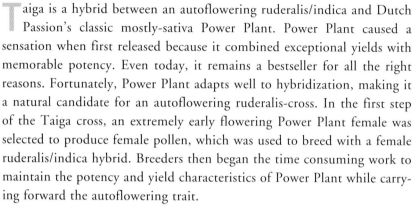

even head/body, lucid

sweet-spicy

35–49 days

♂ Power Plant x ♀ ruderalis/indica hybrid

25–50g per plant

Taiga is a hybrid between an autoflowering ruderalis/indica and Dutch Passion's classic mostly-sativa Power Plant. Power Plant caused a sensation when first released because it combined exceptional yields with memorable potency. Even today, it remains a bestseller for all the right reasons. Fortunately, Power Plant adapts well to hybridization, making it a natural candidate for an autoflowering ruderalis-cross. In the first step of the Taiga cross, an extremely early flowering Power Plant female was selected to produce female pollen, which was used to breed with a female ruderalis/indica hybrid. Breeders then began the time consuming work to maintain the potency and yield characteristics of Power Plant while carrying forward the autoflowering trait.

Taiga crashes through its growth cycle in a genetically dictated automatic regime. It is a small bushy, but not overly branchy, plant that grows large, compact green buds reminiscent of its Power Plant parent. Average heights are around 2 feet (50–60 cm), although some will stay as short as a foot (30 cm) and the tallest may read 2.5 feet (70 cm).

Indoors Taiga does well under a light cycle of 20 hours on/4 hours off. Whether it is grown inside or in a sunny outdoor environment, Taiga grows from seeds to potent, aromatic, and great looking buds in just 8–10 weeks. Half-gallon (1.5–2 liter) containers are sufficient for a good harvest. Even outdoor growers with the shortest of summers will find that this productive new strain performs. Taiga is robust enough to make the most of the growing conditions with which it is presented. It is undemanding when it comes to the fertilizing regime, making it a good choice for beginners, who can often struggle with more exacting nutrient requirements. While plants always benefit from good nutrients and light, this variety still thrives when handed less than optimal conditions.

The sweet-spicy smell and rich taste of Taiga are similar to Power Plant. The high blends a gentle combination of physical relaxation and an "up" cerebral element. Many smokers appreciate a well-rounded high that can be savored and appreciated, rather than a whopping stone that requires cautious intake to avoid incapacitation. Taiga is potent yet stays pleasant and happy, allowing one freedom in choosing what to do with it. Taiga's ease and swiftness in the garden and its functional effects make this strain an all-around pleasant experience.

The Kali
Big Buddha Seeds

Kali, the dark and fierce Hindu goddess, is a powerful force, bringing change. In the yin-yang of Eastern cultures, this goddess is both destructive and creative, nurturing and protecting her children, but also defending them with violent ferocity. In Tantric beliefs, Kali is a dominating force, foremost among the goddesses. Her name in Tantra expands to also mean the original form of all things, or ultimate reality. Kali is usually portrayed as a many-armed dark-skinned blue or black goddess with glittering eyes and a fearsome extended tongue.

The strain known as "The Kali" originates from the Afghani/Pakistani border. It is a landrace OG Kush that was selfed with a reversed Kali clone father taken from seeds whose male was responsible for the original backcross that led to the Cup-winning Big Buddha Cheese. Kali is from old-school indica parents, the real hashmaking deal from the home of ancient hashmaking tradition, an area that has selected for hash excellence among its plants over generations upon generations.

The Kali is a dark fierce-growing indica that has thin dark green leaflets and very little but very sturdy branching, especially for such an indica-influenced plant. She likes moderate to heavy feeding and will do well in any substrate from soil or coco to hydro. The Kali is not a large plant, usually entering flower at 2 feet (70 cm) and finishing between 4–6 feet (1.3–2 meters). The Kali stands up well to heat or cold and is good for growers at all levels of experience. The yields on this plant are good indoors or out, with each plant easily delivering a kilogram (2.2 pounds) if treated with respect. The buds are conical and as resinous as you'd expect from a hash-derived variety.

The Kali has a dark hash smell in the garden and throws out buds like fat feathered goddess tongues. The buds glisten with rich layers of THC, the dense ambrosia of this goddess plant. Kali is an obvious choice for hashmaking. Cured buds will also have a very hashish-like flavor and aroma, dense and smooth, with a unique, earthy citrus-kush richness. This is slow trajectory pot, with a flow of euphoria and creeper body stoniness. The Kali is the manifestation of Kundalini energy, which is one's dormant energy force that lies at the base of the spine and, when awoken, restores vitality. Kali brings awakening in her dark tasty form, and her delights will make her a savored addition to any collection.

 80/20

 sedative, stoney, intense

 lemon-lime, kush

 56–70 days

 ♂♀ OG landrace

 500g per m² in 1000g per m² out

 SOG

The OG #18
DNA/Reserva Privada

spacey, couchlock

fuel/sour

63 days

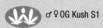
♂♀ OG Kush S1

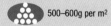
500–600g per m²

SOG

The OG #18 was selected from a set of the original feminized OG Kush seeds. After a little time with the OG #18, it was clear that she was a keeper phenotype with many good and winning qualities, leading DNA to feminize her. Compared with the original OG Kush, this strain takes on a more sour taste reminiscent of the fuel-sour tones of the Chem Dawg, but with the OG-Chem power.

The OG #18 also makes better use of the space than her predecessors, averaging better yields than OG Kush—a third more on average. This plant branches a lot and will stretch a little during the vegetative phase, but when the roots hit bottom, OG #18 growth takes off, spreading out into a bush and doubling in size. DNA recommends pinching to direct growth. The buds are bigger than the OG Kush, and they get rock hard as the plant nears ripeness. Beware of spider mites as they seem to be attracted to the OG #18, but even with the compact bud structures, molds aren't a problem. These plants bounce back from nutrient faux pas easier than some. However, OG #18 will become unhappy in hot rooms or climates. At 9 weeks, The OG #18 buds are mature and become little beauties that twinkle with a sheen of resin.

The OG #18 is a musky strain that gives off a scent from the get-go, and the odor only gets more intense during the flowering period. The final cured buds transform this muskiness into a tasty Kush flavor with a sour undertone. The high is long lasting and trancey. The OG #18 is tunnel vision pot that washes out peripheral vision. The high feels like a bubble has been stretched around you. When the bubble pops, it is as if the high caused time to warp. The clock doesn't seem to match the perception of how much time has passed. These qualities make OG #18 optimal for focused leisure such as playing video games, but a terrible idea for driving or staying on schedule. The OG #18 won the 2009/2010 *High Times* Cannabis Cup in the Indica Category for the Reserva Privada series. She also won the 2010 Europe Champions Cup and 2010 Spannabis Indoor Hydro Cup.

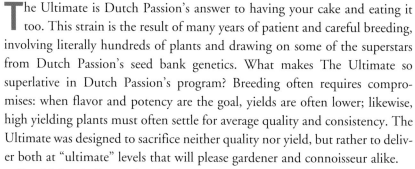

The Ultimate
Dutch Passion

The Ultimate is Dutch Passion's answer to having your cake and eating it too. This strain is the result of many years of patient and careful breeding, involving literally hundreds of plants and drawing on some of the superstars from Dutch Passion's seed bank genetics. What makes The Ultimate so superlative in Dutch Passion's program? Breeding often requires compromises: when flavor and potency are the goal, yields are often lower; likewise, high yielding plants must often settle for average quality and consistency. The Ultimate was designed to sacrifice neither quality nor yield, but rather to deliver both at "ultimate" levels that will please gardener and connoisseur alike.

Combining indica and sativa genetics to create a high quality 50/50 offspring is more difficult than many would expect. The challenge is to fully stabilize characteristics such as height, yield, and the consistency of the stone. Beyond its even balance of indica and sativa, the details of The Ultimate's genetic heritage remain a closely guarded Dutch Passion secret.

 50/50

 potent, stoney, relaxing

 rich citrus haze

 56–70 days

 undisclosed indica and sativa

 550g per m² in 400–500g per plant out

 in/greenhouse preferred

The Ultimate grows into a dense stout and resilient plant, reaching average heights of 2–2.5 feet (60–75 cm) at finish. The short stature is ideally suited to the indoor grower who wants big yields of top-drawer stash but has space limitations. This plant's uniform growth habits lead to an even canopy in the grow room or greenhouse, which helps to maximize light exposure. Moderate to strong nutrients are recommended during the vegetative phase to help beef up stem sturdiness. This pine-tree shaped plant is best grown with multiple branches, which should be supported due to the stem-breaking heft of its buds. The Ultimate's hybrid foliage is neither fat nor thin, and may gain red or blue hues as the plants finish. Inexperienced growers should not get too impatient because there is an exceptional growth spurt during the last two weeks of flowering that pumps up the yield. These sticky crystal-covered plants exude a strong sweet aroma that may require stealth measures. While it can make nice finger hash, accidental brushing against plants leaves a strong odor on clothes for hours afterwards.

The Ultimate delivers a stone of the highest order. Delicious hints of orange citrus shine through. The flavor sensation is almost tropical and very rich, and the experienced smoker may detect a touch of haze flavors. The high is a heavy-hitter that is best served when relaxing, rather than when activities are on the menu. Friends may want to caution the occasional toker about this strain's high potency before they inhale. Growers and seasoned smokers are likely to find that this strain lives up to its name in terms of its sizeable stash and its connoisseur smoke.

The Story Behind the Ultimate

Dutch Passion breeders pride themselves on having exacting standards. They seek out high-quality genetics and then look for outstanding individual plants among the hundreds that are grown out. The selected individuals serve as the basis for Dutch Passion's breeding program, so they must possess the qualities that lead to superb varieties. A lot of discernment goes into every Dutch Passion selection. So when breeders were visibly excited over the variety that became "The Ultimate," everyone was curious to find out why. It was a good sign that this variety had bountiful yields worthy of enthusiasm. But the true test would be in the "blind" testing trials.

Testing trials are "blind" tests because the smoker does not know the identity of the strain they receive. This is to ensure that their assessments are not biased by associating the variety name with their experience. This allows new strains to be compared against known, "standard" strains. It's a tough job, but someone has to do it! In this instance, Dutch Passion calls on the expertise of some highly experienced Dutch smoke-testers who are skilled in discerning the good from the outstanding.

When the smoke testers got hold of this strain, they were just as passionate as the breeders had been, declaring that the potency and excellent taste were top-shelf. Ever cautious and skeptical, the strain was evaluated again without any other strains that might influence the assessment. Again, the testers were adamant: this was a special strain. Several of them started calling it "the ultimate" variety, and the name stuck.

Time and time again in controlled smoke trials, The Ultimate has been voted most potent. It is this feedback that has convinced Dutch Passion that the variety deserves its name. In terms of yield, this plant is in the top 10% of what can be achieved. This yield potential combined with the high quality stash has convinced Dutch Passion that The Ultimate is "quite possibly the most important strain our breeders have ever created."

Titan's Haze
Flying Dutchmen

Photo left: Soft Secrets Magazine

The Titans in Greek mythology were the powerful elder deities that ruled during the Golden Age. Most Titans were associated with primal elements—the ocean, earth, sun, and moon. Long after their reign, they left their mark on the world through their continued presence in the most basic and primitive aspects of the world's composition. Titan's Haze is a variety that unearths and carries forward certain elder deities from the marijuana kingdom's golden age.

The Original Haze genetics in this cross are a direct descendant of the Haze Brothers California creation in the 1980s, a blend of Mexican, Colombian, Thai, and south Indian strains that has a distinct connoisseur flavor and high often sought after and frequently hybridized into contemporary strains. The Flying Dutchmen's Skunk #1 (the Pure) strain is the unadulterated progeny of the 1970s California Skunk #1. A hybrid of Columbian, Mexican, and Afghan landrace strains, the Skunk #1 is a sweet smelling plant that has balanced growth for a sativa-dominant plant. Titan's sister plant from Flying Dutchmen, the Fuma con Diablos, reverses the cross with a Skunk #1 mother and an Original Haze father.

Titan's Haze was created in a greenhouse and is best suited for indoor or greenhouse cultivation in soil, but can be grown outdoors in long-season equatorial climates such as Spain and southern California. Novice growers who long for sativa stash should not shy away from this versatile Haze. She can be grown in small personal gardens or in a sea of green with little or no previous experience. Flying Dutchmen recommends limited vegetative time and 20 plants per square meter in a sea of green setup. The Titan's Haze growth pattern is slender with a typical haze structure—wide, evenly distributed nodal spacing on moderate, graceful branches. The light green calyxes turn golden toward harvest and build to form swollen teardrop-shaped colas that outweigh many commonly grown haze varieties, with possible outdoor yields of over a kilo per plant in their homeland equatorial climate. These plants are good in high humidity or dry climates and have proven resistant to pests and molds.

When entering a room in which the Titan's Haze has been smoked, the fragrant yet slightly acrid grassy smell will make mouths water with hopes for the impending high. The taste is less sweet than many hybrids, a return to an old-school haze profile. Titan's Haze brings back the legendary cerebral rush that sativa connoisseurs crave. The buzz soars with mildly trippy effects on heavier use, and a stimulating, creative impulse that endears it to artists and musicians. This is accompanied by a hint of Afghani body hit. Its powerful buzz is energizing and good for ADHD, but it may bring out a manic tendency in a naturally hyperactive person. Use caution when mixing pleasures—combined with alcoholic beverages, the potency may become unpleasant. Occasional users should show restraint to maximize enjoyment. More experienced sativa fans will delight in the ecstatic, clean, enduring high from this haze Titan.

 85/15

 soaring, trippy

 acrid, grassy

 84–98 days

 ♂ The Original Haze x ♀ Skunk #1 (the Pure)

 0.5–1 g per watt of light in
1000 g per plant out

 in preferred

SOG

Tora Bora
DNA/Reserva Privada

 body stone

 hashy kush

 56–63 days

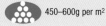 ♂LA Confidential x ♀X-18 pure Pakistani

 450–600g per m²

The Tora Bora is a peaceful meeting of pure Pakistani and pure Afghani. This cross of two legendary indicas results in a great stash of bluish-green knockout nuggs for the high tolerance smoker.

The award-winning LA Confidential mother strain originated from an Affie clone. She is known for being a dark, dank green plant that grows slowly in vegetative phase and produces modest per-plant yields of connoisseur, heavy Kush favored indica tastiness. The Pakistani X-18 father is an early stretching plant that slows to a more indica pattern in flowering and finishes with chunky pungent blue-hued nuggets. Both parent plants are known as strong medicinal indicas with a history of relieving pain and helping patients with insomnia. The combination of the two results in a vigorous, fast finishing plant that is crystal coated with good medicine.

Average yields of the Tora Bora improve on the mother and make this variety a good candidate for small gardens as well as larger grows. This is a plant for the indica flavor fan, and to bring out the most, soil and organics deliver better flavor intensity. The Tora Bora plant has the typical wide, dark foliage of an indica and forms one main cola, with average side branching. Pinching or topping will help with yields. This plant can handle cold weather as long as there is no frost. Final heights will only be about 1 1/2 times the height at flower forcing, so breeders recommend these plants vegetate for as long as possible to help beef up size and yield. Tora Bora will gobble up nutrients like a fat lady at an all-you-can-eat buffet. She isn't particularly sensitive about nutrient levels and is fairly forgiving, making her a good strain for a novice grower to learn on. However, the potent indica punch of the final product may make this strain more intriguing for medicinal indica users or veteran indica smokers who know they want big body stone effects.

The smell of the Tora Bora is not overwhelming when it is growing, but the buds get so Velcro-sticky with resin that even barely brushing against one will superglue down arm hair, and release aromas as you tug free. Tora Bora delivers a pleasing yield of greenish-blue and hashy-sweet indica depth. This strain will bring on a strong body relaxation and may cause some conspicuous eye droop. Medicinally, it is good for insomnia.

Tropi-canna
Seeds of Freedom

Photos: Breeder D

Tropi-canna is a playful shorthand for "tropical cannabis," bringing to mind the lavish, sultry luxury of tropical settings known as enviable vacation destinations and global sweet spots for cultivating kind bud. It was the lush tropical qualities of this variety that inspired its Tropi-canna name.

This variety is the progeny of a Sensi Star F2 female and a Hawaiian Skunk daddy. As a hybrid, Tropi-canna adopts its flowering time and growth pattern from its indica roots while possessing sativa qualities in taste, smell, and effects. This plant can be grown in either hydro or soil, although soil will bring out more of the mango-haze treats in its flavor. Tropi-canna is a slow starter, but branches well and fares best as a screen of green or multi-branch plant. Sea of green methods can also work successfully if the bottom branches are trimmed.

These dark green plants could easily blend into lavish equatorial gardens, but they can also be grown in outdoor gardens beyond the tropics belt, where they will finish by the end of September in latitudes equivalent with southern Ontario, Canada. The leaves show a sativa influence, with many slender leaflets. As they grow, there is a slight internode stretch. Tropi-canna is a natural mama who prefers lower nutrients: even better if they're organic. By the end of flowering, she is typically doubled in size from what it was at forcing. Plants are best forced at 12–18 inches, resulting in average final plants that are 30–36 inches tall.

Tropi-canna plants are aromatic as they vegetate, but the smell becomes lighter and less conspicuous during flowering. In the second half of the flower cycle, these plants go through a transformation, exploding with bud growth and resin production until even the leaf petioles are covered in glands. Ha-cha-cha! Or perhaps Hash—Uh-huh! This plant should definitely be considered a serious contender for bubble hash processing.

Tropi-canna buds at finish have an amazing and distinct tropical flavor, a mixture of fresh melon, citrusy lemon, and the flowery edge of haze—sorry, no orange juice in this Tropi-canna treat. The high invokes a giddy and decadent sense of enjoyment. Tropi-canna encourages a fun and exuberant mood that would fit right in to the ambiance of an island vacation.

 65/35

 energetic, happy, talkative, uplifting

 tropical mango-lemon haze

 55–60 days

 ♀Sensi Star F2 x ♂Hawaiian Skunk

 400–500g per m² 25–30g per plant SOG: 40–60g per plant SCROG

 SOG

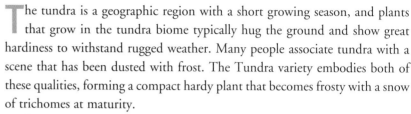

Tundra
Dutch Passion

balanced, relaxed

sweet citrus

56–77 days

Passion #1 x ruderalis

25–50g per plant

The tundra is a geographic region with a short growing season, and plants that grow in the tundra biome typically hug the ground and show great hardiness to withstand rugged weather. Many people associate tundra with a scene that has been dusted with frost. The Tundra variety embodies both of these qualities, forming a compact hardy plant that becomes frosty with a snow of trichomes at maturity.

This autoflowering variety was developed from the champion Dutch Passion outdoor strain, Passion #1. Passion #1 is a variety that originated in California during the 1970s, and was refined to become a sturdy pest- and disease-resistant outdoor indica strain. Dutch Passion started a breeding program to introduce the autoflowering ruderalis to traditional strains, and found that some gave especially strong results, Passion #1 among them. Breeders worked carefully to formulate an autoflowering version of the Passion #1, utilizing ruderalis and other strains as needed to stabilize a hybrid that retains the desirable potency and balanced high of the Passion #1 with the genetics to flower automatically without a carefully controlled light regimen.

This healthy, easygoing variety can be grown almost anywhere. Outdoors, Tundra seeds can be planted as early as the start of spring or as late as August and will automatically start and complete the flowering process, leaving you the proud owner of a Tundra harvest in 56–77 days from the time the seed sprouts until the buds are finished. Tundra will also deliver excellent results indoors under a cycle of 20 hours light /4 hours darkness. The genetics from Passion #1 have passed on an excellent resistance to mold and bud rot.

Tundra grows into a compact, strong, and vibrantly green bush with limited branching. It stays short and matures quickly, growing vegetatively for just over 2 weeks when it reaches a height around 2 feet (50cm). Then Tundra automatically enters flowering, which takes an additional 6–9 weeks. Plants finish at heights of around 3 feet (80 cm) with an average yield of 1–2 ounces (25–50g) per plant.

The Tundra buds are firm and rich in THC crystals. The high is a pleasurable blend of body relaxation and moderate "up" effects. If you plunge your nose into a baggie of buds, the aroma is thick and sweet with a citrus edge. The soft smoke smells of spices mixed with an astringent fruity quality of lemons and grapefruits. Tundra allows one to drift freely in a happy state of relaxation, translating well to a calm enjoyment while socializing with friends or to leisurely solo activities such as a peaceful afternoon in a hammock.

Urban Poison
Nirvana

D on't be frightened away by this strain's ominous name. Urban Poison is a new indoor version of the famous Durban Poison from South Africa. The famed Durban Poison is mostly sativa landrace. In this strain, Nirvana has crossed Durban Poison with Northern Lights and then backcrossed the hybrid with the parent Durban Poison again. The result is a mostly sativa variety that retains the juniper flavor and trippy high of its South African parent.

The Urban Poison structure and potency is that of modern indoor production strains: uniform, stable, and compact. The leaves are medium to thin with light green tones and lots of leaflets. As it grows, Urban Poison takes on the characteristic Christmas-tree shape. The sativa dominance is offset by a significant blend of indica, making it a fairly robust plant that is easy to grow and accommodating of temperature fluctuations within reason. These plants do well in soil, and given the minimal branching, they conform well to a sea of green setup. Organics are recommended to bring out the depth of flavors.

 60/40

 cheerful, even head/body

 juniper, woodsy, licorice

 60 days

 ♀Durban Poison x ♂NL

 400–500g per m²

While this variety is well adapted to indoor gardens, it is a fine choice for outdoor gardens. When planted in May, it finishes by the end of October. Outdoor plants will gain ²/₃ of their final height during the flowering phase, with maximum sizes of 9 feet (3 meters).

The Urban Poison buds are rather tight, long, and spongy. The smell is strong but has accents that distinguish it from the average strain. The fresh pine and juniper smells remind one of the smells in the forest, walking under a canopy of high cedar trees where pine needles blanket the ground.

Once cured, Urban Poison buds crumble nicely and burn evenly. The up effect creeps into consciousness and then through the body, with a long lifespan to the high. This is an urban brain safari. It has a cheerful alert quality that is great for energetic activities such as dancing, playing soccer or Frisbee, or cleaning anything. Many people will find something special in the deep woodsy aroma and flavor that has just a touch of haze.

Vanilla Kush
Barney's Farm

Vanilla Kush brings out creamy vanilla flavors in this pure indica Kush. The mother is a hash plant from Kashmir, a valley in the Himalayas of the northwestern Indian subcontinent. This region is a traditional hashmaking region, and the mother plant is a landrace variety of high quality coming from the cannabis motherlands. The cross is with a Hindu Kush father, a landrace strain of Afghanistan origin. When combined, these two heritage strains create a flavorful and highly potent kush.

Landrace kush strains are consistent plants with a strong, steady growth pattern. Vanilla Kush likes to branch and typically forms eight symmetrical side branches. This variety delivers happier, more abundant yields when cultivated as multi-branch plants. The solid growth adapts well to hydro and soil systems, and thrives when a SCROG setup is used. When grown indoors, plants typically finish at a height of around 2 feet (60cm) and take roughly 9 weeks to flower. Outdoors, these plants finish at the end of September. With two months' flowering time, outdoor plants can yield up to 8 ounces (250g) apiece.

Vanilla Kush is an iconic, medium-dark plant that stays green throughout and only fades in color as the buds finish. The leaves have thick velvety leaflets with a heavy sugar coating of trichomes hugging close to the leaf base. The glands darken into little globules of red and gold as the plant reaches maturity, and the hairs take on a bright burnished orange hue. Kushes are known to form large, sturdy, and dense colas, and Vanilla Kush is no different. It is notably distinct due to its intensely rich aromas, mixing herbal smells of lavender with the deeper tones of vanilla bean and some acrid accents of citrus peel.

Vanilla Kush placed second in the 2009 overall Cannabis Cup, an accolade that speaks to its appealing combination of creamy flavors and potent effect. Kushes are known for their high THC levels, and this variety delivers a potent and long lasting high that is particularly strong in its physical effects. Vanilla Kush is also a standout on taste. The strong, sweet herbal-floral notes dominate the smoke. This variety induces a strong sense of relaxation, easing muscle tension, which appeals to many medical marijuana users. In smaller amounts, the mental effect is euphoric and thoughtful, yet relaxed. Heavy indulgence strengthens the effects, leading to a trippy and potentially sleepy tunnel vision that may cause couchlock or napping.

 I

 relaxed, trippy

 vanilla musk

 60–65 days

 ♀Kashmir x ♂Afghani

 40g per plant in 100–200g per plant out

183

Vanilluna
DJ Short

Vanilluna—aka "Vanilla Moon"—is a Kush-like quasi-hybrid named for its complex yet subtle creamy vanilla-honeyed palate. This Oregon strain's parents are both Blueberry in origin. The mother was selected from the Blueberry Sativa line, the same seed stock that produced both Blue Satellite and Cocoa Kush. Vanilluna's particular mother has the characteristics of being larger, mostly green, and symmetric with a distinct dominant main stem, compact nodes, little variegation, and long side branches. It was crossed with DJ Short's Original Blueberry male, an infamous euphoric berry strain that is an indica-dominant hybrid from Thai and Afghan origins.

Even though both parents derive from Blueberry, the Original Blueberry is an indica type, while the mother is a sativa type, making Vanilluna closer to an F1 hybrid than an inbred line. Because of their quasi-F1 status, Vanilluna plants present interesting opportunities, making them valuable breed-stock for collectors of high quality seeds with unique traits. There is a broad spectrum of quality genetic diversity still contained within, waiting to be coaxed free.

Vanilluna grows to be a medium-tall Kush-like plant with short nodes, uniform growth, large, dark green foliage, and thick yet sturdy hollow stems. The Vanilluna buds grow tight and dense, elongating to form spade-shaped colas. As the flowers take shape over their 8–9 weeks, the calyxes and bracts become completely coated in a sheen of clear trichomes with superior aromatics. Don't be tempted to harvest too early; the Vanilluna develops the more interesting oils in the very last week of maturity. In order to optimize yields, an extended vegetative time coupled with early topping is recommended. They can also be run un-topped in a sea of green-type system for good production. At finish, this resin-laden plant is a natural selection for some unique, ultra-potent hash.

Vanilluna possesses flavors that are smooth and creamy with a sweet vanilla taste and a hint of floral bouquet and sweet melon musk. The experience is top-shelf quality, with a comfortable entry and an enduring dreamy effect that induces calmness and clarity. It is a good variety for relaxation and reducing anxiety, a tasty treat for the palate, and a bubble bath for the nerves.

 50/50

 relaxing, mellow, dreamy

 creamy, melon, vanilla

 56–63 days

 ♀ Blueberry Sativa x ♂ Original Blueberry

 1g per watt

SOG

Veryberry (remix)
Humboldt Seed Organisation

Veryberry is a sativa heavy strain selected for its uplifting high and density of berry fruit flavors. The mother is a little known but well loved strawberry haze originating in Switzerland. The father is a mostly-sativa Blueberry variant that includes genetics from Thailand and Mexico. This Blueberry has been circulating in the UK for the last 15 years.

Veryberry was developed as an indoor strain, but it can also be grown outdoors in locations with a long warm autumn that provides a full five month season from spring to fall of non-freezing outdoor weather. This strain shows its sativa heritage from the outset, with medium branching that stretches wide and forms a broad, loose Christmas tree structure. The leaves are slender and light green with a waxy shine.

Although this plant can be tolerant to some variation in conditions, Veryberry is a sativa-dominant strain and has exacting preferences to thrive. Because of this, it is better as a strain for a more experienced grower than for a beginner. Still, compared with many sativas, this strain recovers well when unfavorable conditions have been restored within range. This plant does best as a multi-branch plant, and averages 5 ounces per plant when grown in multi-branch sizes. Plants forced at 12 inches grow to about 3 feet at finish. Maximum yields can be achieved in a flood and drain system, or a system with a high pressure dripper run to waste.

Smells of strawberries fill the garden when Veryberry is flowering, but the odor does not range into the strong dankness that is often a telltale sign of indoor cannabis. At finish the light green buds are covered with lots of orange hairs and are fairly easy to manicure. The cured buds sing with fruity sweet fresh berry and strawberry aromas, and these tones carry over into its berry floral flavors. Veryberry's effects are more high than stoned. This pleasantly awake, happy and energetic sensation builds up gradually into a soaring yet functional state of bliss. It is good for fun with friends, in the sunny outdoors or at home playing videogames and chilling. This high has a trajectory that eventually winds down to a drowsy, dreamy state.

 85/15

 up, blissful, creeper

 fruity sweet strawberry

 4–5 oz. per plant

 ♀ Swiss Strawberry Haze x ♂ Hindu Kush

 56 days

 in preferred

Vortex
TGA Seeds

Welcome to the vortex, a mental house of mirrors in the marijuana kingdom. This mind-bending cross was bred by Subcool from his favorite old and new headstash. The mother is the Apollo 13 and the father is a Space Queen. After testing many hybrids of these strains, the pungent sour-sweet Vortex hybrid was selected. It is a heavily resinous bubble hash strain with a potent, racing high that leans heavily on the more psychedelic spectrum of the cannabis realm.

When left untopped, Vortex forms the classic tree shape, but plants deliver the best yields when topped early and trained to form multiple growing heads. This variety wilts noticeably during the dark period, almost appearing to need watering. Gardeners should remove heavy low side branches to focus the plant's energy on its uppermost shoots. When plants are topped and placed into flowering at 3 feet (1 meter), they finish well under 5 feet (1.75 meters) but will be very wide. This plant is ideal for a SCROG garden. Using these methods can deliver an average of 5 ounces (150g) per plant in soil, and more in hydro systems. Subcool prefers organic nutrients to arrive at the best taste and cleanest ash.

Outdoors, Vortex matures more quickly than the typical sativa, resisting late season mildew. Good reports have been reported for many different types of gardening environments from various parts of the world, so long as the grow season allows the plant to flower for a full 8 weeks. Lots of stakes and string are recommended, since the outdoor Vortex plant grows into a wide sagging bush with hundreds of bud sites that benefit from support.

These plants become bright green with vivid red pistils that fade to a more muted rusty brown as the flowers ripen. The many triangle-shaped, hard and dense buds give the plant a redbud look. The leaves definitely lean toward the sativa, growing blade-thin with a coating of small raised trichomes. Vortex clones easily, but is also very uniform when grown from seeds, with almost no phenotypic variation. The females are nearly identical in smell, taste, and growth characteristics.

The Vortex buzz can be energizing and heart racing, but it can also be ripped under, curled under stupid stoned. This high has virtually no ceiling, so that the high keeps climbing without a burnout point. When used lightly, this strain is a real pick-up for the senses, stoking creative juices and provoking thought. With heavier use, Vortex becomes mentally confusing and potentially disorienting. Even veterans can find themselves spinning and swirling in the vortex of its psychedelic influences.

This strain may take discipline due to its sweet-tart aromas and flavors that leave one's lips smack-

 80/20

 speedy, mindbending

 pineapple and peach baby food

 56 days

 ♀Apollo 13 x ♂Space Queen

 150g per plant

 in preferred

g for another taste. Some have compared the smell to a mango ink with tart lemonade overtones. The flavor has a similar mix smooth fruit flavors, likened to peach baby food, mixed with sweet astringency reminiscent of pineapple. Vortex is definitely zzying headstash of the highest rank, and has also gained a fol-lowing from those who use marijuana medically for chronic pain because it assuages physical pain but also calms many of the emo-tions that accompany the experience of chronic pain.

1st place, 2010 *High Times* Medicinal Cup, San Francisco

Whitaker Blues
DJ Short

Whitaker Blues is a true Oregon heritage cross developed by DJ Short's son, JD. The mother of this strain is currently referred to as "Quimby"; an old-school West Coast staple reminiscent of a classic, early indica lineage. Quimby is strong and sleepy in its effect. The father is Blueberry, also originating from the West Coast of the US, mixing Oaxaca, Thai, and Afghani genetics.

This West Coast marriage makes Whitaker Blues an indica-dominant strain, and the indica background is prominent in its growth characteristics. This strain is a stout, short-branching hybrid that sports large, compact and highly resinous buds. Whitaker's growth is both vigorous and productive, performing well in either hydro or soil and proving resilient to many minor garden fluctuations. It finishes after 55–62 days of flowering, and hues of violet and blue creep in toward the end of the flowering cycle. At finish, Whitaker Blues plants are medium-short in stature with thick leaves and large, chunky buds.

Whitaker Blues has a complex and enchanting smell that ranges from pungent to sweet. One may get hints of a floral berry candy, a more astringent grapefruit citrus, a honeyed sweetness, or a musky pungency. The flavor is both pungent and sweet, with a distinct velvety grape flavor and a mild suggestion of vanilla.

This variety mixes the high profiles of its parents in sequence, beginning with a strong initial stimulating and slightly giddy effect that increases inspiration, sensuality, and appetite, leading to munchies. This is followed by the Quimby's more sedate, dreamy sensations that may make napping or daydreaming much more enticing.

 80/20

 munchies, stoney, dreamy

 floral grapefruit honey

 55–62 days

 ♀Quimby x ♂Blueberry

 1g per watt

SOG

Alaskan Ice • AMS • Anesthesia • Angelma

Blue Cheese • Barney's Farm G13-Haze

Haze • Carnival • Cataract Kush • CH9 Fl

• Chiesel • Cocoa Kush • Crippled Pit

Dark Star • DelaHaze • Diabolic Funxt

Haze • Easy Rider • Funxta'z Purple C

Headband • Herijuana • Himalaya Gold

#5 • Jamaican Pearl • Jock Horror • K-Tr

• L.A.P.D. • Lemon Skunk • LSD • Mar

Morning Star • Mr. Nice • Northern Ligh

• Pit Bull • PolarLight • Purple Voodo

• Skunk Haze • Sleestack • Smoothie

Southern Nights • Super Lemon Haze •

Kali • The OG #18 • The Ultimate • Titar

• Urban Poison • Vanilla Kush Vanillu

Apollo 13BX • Automaria • Barney's Farm

Black Berry • Bubble Cheese • Buddha

er • CH9 G Bolt • CH9 Jack 33 • Cheesus

Critical #47 • Crystalberry • Dancehall

Dr. Grinspoon • Dready Kush • Dutch

Kush • G-Bomb • Green House Thai •

ranian Autoflower • Jack F6 • Jack Flash

• Kandahar • Killing Fields • Kushadelic

a #1 • Mekong High • Morning Glory •

Apollo G13 • NYPD • Oregon Pinot Noir

Qleaner • Querkle • Raspberry Cough

nowStorm • Soma-licious • Somantra •

iss Cheese • Tahoe Gold • Taiga • The

aze • Tora Bora • Tropi-canna • Tundra

• Veryberry • Vortex • Whitaker Blues

Appendixes

Seed Companies & Varieties

Barney's Farm
Barneys Farm Blue Cheese
Barney's Farm G-13 Haze
Dr. Grinspoon
LSD
Morning Glory
Vanilla Kush

The Netherlands
www.barneys.biz

Big Buddha Seeds
Bubble Cheese
Buddha Haze
Cheesus
Chiesel
G-Bomb
The Kali

PO Box 12822
B32 9BB
United Kingdom
salesteam@bigbuddhaseeds.com
www.bigbuddhaseeds.com

Biotops/Queen Seeds
Northern Light x Apollo G13

Spain
www.queen-seeds.com

California Bean Bank
L.A.P.D.
Purple Voodoo
Smoothie

Berkeley, CA
USA
+1 888.420.2326
info@beanbank.com
www.beanbank.com

CH9 Female Seeds
CH9 Flower
CH9 G Bolt
CH9 Jack 33

Spain
ch9care@gmail.com
www.ch9femaleseeds.com

Coffeeshop Classics by Ceres Seeds
Easy Rider
Skunk Haze

PO Box 10213
1001 EE Amsterdam
The Netherlands
+31 020.773.7014
info@ceresseeds.com
www.ceresseeds.com

DJ Short
Cocoa Kush
Vanilluna
Whitaker Blues

USA/Canada
www.greatcanadianseeds.com
www.legendseeds.com

DNA Genetics/Reserva Privada
Cataract Kush
Headband
Lemon Skunk
Sleestack
The OG #18
Tora Bora

Sint Nicolaasstraat 41
1012 NJ Amsterdam
The Netherlands
+31 020.778.7220
info@dnagenetics.com
www.dnagenetics.com

Don't Panic Organix
Diabolic Funxta
Funxta'z Purple Cali Kush

USA
info@dontpanicorganix.com
dontpanicorganix@yahoo.com
www.dontpanicorganix.com

Dutch Passion
Dutch Haze
Mekong High
PolarLight
SnowStorm
Taiga
The Ultimate
Tundra

Dutch Passion Wholesale Amsterdam/
Head Office
Hoogoorddreef 109
1101 BB Amsterdam
Netherlands
www.dutchpassion.nl

Fast Seed Bank
Southern Nights

Spain
info@fastseedbank.com
www.fastseedbank.com

Flying Dutchmen
Titan's Haze

The Netherlands
info@flyingdutchmen.com
www.flyingdutchmen.com

Green House Seed Company
Alaskan Ice
AMS
Green House Thai
Himalaya Gold

Green House Seed Company (con't.)
K-Train
Super Lemon Haze

O.Z. Voorburgwal 191
1012 EA Amsterdam
The Netherlands
+31 020.716.3834
orders@greenhouse.org
www.greenhouseseeds.nl
www.kingofcannabis.com

Greenthumb Seeds
Iranian Autoflower

Box 37085
Ottawa, Ontario K1V 0W9
Canada
+ 1 613.330.2404
drgreenthumb@drgreenthumb.com
www.drgreenthumb.com

Humboldt Seed Organisation
Dready Kush
Veryberry (remix)

UK
info@humboldtseeds.co.uk
www.humboldtseeds.co.uk

Mandala Seeds
Mandala #1

Spain
info@mandalaseeds.com
www.mandalaseeds.com

Master Thai Organics
Tahoe Gold

P.O. Box 16538
South Lake Tahoe, CA 96151
United States of America
+1 530.314.1383
master_thaigardens@yahoo.com
www.masterthai.com

Ministry of Cannabis
Angelmatic
Carnival
Kandahar

Postbus 460
1500 EL Zaandam
The Netherlands
info@ministryofcannabis.com
www.ministryofcannabis.com

Nirvana
Black Berry
Jock Horror
NYPD (New York Power Diesel)
Raspberry Cough
Swiss Cheese
Urban Poison

The Netherlands
info@nirvana.nl
www.nirvana.nl

Paradise Seeds

Automaria
DelaHaze

PO Box 377
1000 AJ Amsterdam
The Netherlands
+31 20.679.5422
info@paradise-seeds.com
www.paradise-seeds.com

Positronics Seeds SL

Critical #47

C/Ronda De Las Ventas, 4 Bajo
31600, Burlada, Navarra
Spain
+34 0.94.838.5422
info@positronicseeds.com
www.positronicseeds.com

Reggae Seeds

Dancehall

Spain
info@reggaeseeds.com
www.reggaeseeds.com

Sannie's Seeds

Anesthesia
Herijuana
Jack F6
Killing Fields

The Netherlands
whazzup@xs4all.nl
www.sanniesshop.com

Seeds of Freedom

Crystalberry
Morning Star
Tropi-canna

Canada
seeds-of-freedom@hotmail.com
www.seeds-of-freedom.com

Sensi Seed Bank

Jack Flash #5
Jamaican Pearl
Mr. Nice

P.O. Box 10952
1001 EZ, Amsterdam
The Netherlands
+31 020.626.2988
info@sensiseeds.com
www.sensiseeds.com

Soma's Sacred Seeds

Kushadelic
Soma-licious
Somantra

The Netherlands
soma@somaseeds.nl
www.somaseeds.nl

Stoney Girl Gardens

Crippled Pit
Oregon Pinot Noir
Pit Bull

10117 SE Sunnyside Rd., Ste F 1198
Happy Valley, OR 97015
USA
+1 503.788.2349
info@gro4me.com
www.gro4me.com

TGA Seeds

Apollo 13BX
Qleaner
Querkle
Vortex

USA
www.tgagenetics.com

TH Seeds

Dark Star

The Netherlands
info@thseeds.com
www.thseeds.com

Glossary

aeroponics: growing plants by misting roots that are suspended in air

apical tip: the growing tip of the plant

backcrossing: crossing of an offspring with one of the parents to reinforce a trait

bract: small reduced leaflet in cannabis that appears below a pair of calyxes

calyx: pod harboring the female ovule and two pistils, seed pod

CBC: cannabichromene—one of several non-psychoactive cannabinoids

CBD: cannabidiol—one of several non-psycho-active cannabinoids; it is anti-inflammatory

F1 generation: first filial generation, the off-spring of two parent (P1) plants

F2 generation: second filial generation, the off-spring of two F1 plants

feminized: a seed that will produce only 100% female plants

hydroponics: growing plants in nutrient solu-tion without soil

indica: plant originating in the 30th parallel typified by wide, dark green or purple vegetation; it grows short internodes with profuse branching that forms a wide pyramid shape usually no more than 6 feet tall

internodes: the space between nodes

node: a section of the stem where leaves and side shoots arise; nodes are often swollen, and are sometimes referred to as joints

P1: first parental generation, the parents crossed to form F1 or F1 hybrid offspring

pistils (stigmas): small pair of fuzzy white hairs extending from top of the calyx, designed to capture pollen floating in the air

pollen: the male reproductive product that fertilizes the female flower, a cream-colored or yellow dust released by the male flower which floats along air currents to reach the female

psychoactive: affecting the consciousness or psyche

ruderalis: plant originating from the 50–55th parallel in Russia, typified by the auto flowering of the plant based on age instead of lighting schemes

sativa: plant originating from the 45–50th parallel typified by a tall pine-tree-like growth habit (5 to 15 feet), long internodes, light green color and airy buds

screen of green (SCROG): A technique for supporting plants; a net is secured to a frame and held horizontally so the branches grow through the holes; the nets hold the branches in place so they don't bend or droop and helps support them when they are heavily laden with buds

sea of green (SOG): indoor method for growing marijuana in which many plants are grown close together with little time spent in vegetative growth; rather than a few plants growing large and filling the canopy, many smaller plants are forced into flowering creating a lower canopy and earlier harvest

sepal: a modified leaf located at the base of a flower

stipule: the section where the plant stem meets the leaf stem, or petiole

strain: a line of offspring derived from common ancestors

terpene: class of chemicals composed of repeating units of isoprene (C5H8) to form chains or 3D structures; associated with various scents and may be responsible for the varied highs in cannabis

THC: tetrahydrocannabinol, primary psychoactive component of cannabis

trichome: plant hair that is either glandular (secreting) or eglandular (non secreting)

wpf: watts per square foot

wpm: watts per square meter

When Will Your Outdoor Plants Mature?

C annabis flowers based on the number of hours of uninterrupted dark period it receives. When a critical period is reached for several days the plant changes its growth from vegetative to flowering. During the spring and summer the number of hours of darkness shrinks as the latitude increases. For instance, on June 16, close to June 22, the longest day of the year and the first day of summer, there are 9½ hours of darkness at the 35th latitude, near Memphis, Albuquerque and Los Angeles. At the 40th parallel, close to New York, Columbus and Denver the dark period is 9 hours, a difference of half an hour. However, the seed producer's latitudes are considerably different than the latitudes of the gardens of many outdoor growers. Vancouver, at the 50th parallel and Holland at the 52nd parallel have 7:49 and 7:27 hours of darkness respectively on that date. As a result, maturity dates change significantly with changes in latitude.

To find the ripening date at your latitude:

1. Count back from the outdoor ripening date the number of days the variety takes to flower indoors. This is the trigger date, the date that the plant changes from vegetative to flowering phase.
2. Locate the breeder's latitude at the trigger date. The chart (next page) indicates the number of hours of darkness that trigger the plant to flower.
3. On the column representing your latitude, locate the date on the chart that matches the dark period from #2.
4. Count forward the number of days it takes to ripen indoors. The result is the maturity date.

Figuring Ripening Dates: Examples

A variety from Holland ripens there on October 15 and matures in 70 days indoors. Counting back on the latitude chart you see that on August 1, about 75 days before ripening, the plant triggered on 8½ hours of darkness. Along the 40th parallel or further south, the dark period never gets below 9 hours of darkness. The variety will be triggered to flower almost as soon as it is placed outside. If it's planted outdoors June 1 it will ripen in 70 days, near August 10. If planted June 16 it will ripen in late August. At the 45th parallel, the plant will be triggered to flower around July 1. The buds will mature September 10–15.

A Canadian variety adapted to the 50th parallel ripens October 16 outdoors, 60 days after forcing indoors. Counting back to Aug 16, 60 days before the bud matures, the dark period at the 50th parallel is about 9 ½ hours. At the 45th parallel this dark period occurs August 4, with a ripening date of around October 4. At the 40th parallel it occurs around July 30, with a harvest around September 30. At the 35th parallel and lower latitudes, flowering is triggered as soon as the plants are planted since there are only a few days around June 22 when the dark period stretches longer than 9½ hours. If planted June 1, the plants will ripen in early August.

NUMBER OF HOURS OF DARKNESS BY LATITUDE

Latitude	0	+10	+20	+30	+35	+40	+45	+50	+52	+54	+56	+58
June 16	11:53	11:18	10:40	9:56	9:30	8:59	8:24	7:49	7:27	6:53	6:25	5:53
July 1	11:53	11:18	10:41	9:57	9:31	9:01	8:26	7:41	7:21	6:57	6:29	5:55
July 16	11:53	11:21	10:46	10:08	9:44	9:17	8:45	8:05	7:47	7:25	7:01	7:33
Aug. 1	11:53	11:27	10:59	10:26	10:06	9:44	9:19	8:48	8:32	8:15	7:57	7:35
Aug. 16	11:53	11:34	11:13	10:48	10:33	10:17	9:58	9:35	9:27	9:12	9:59	9:43
Sept. 1	11:53	11:42	11:29	11:15	11:06	10:57	10:45	10:29	10.25	10:18	10:10	10:02
Sept. 16	11:53	11:50	11:46	11:41	11:39	11:35	11:31	11:27	11:24	11:22	11:21	11:16
Oct. 1	11:53	11:59	12:03	12:08	12:11	12:14	12:18	12:22	12:24	12:26	12:28	12:30
Oct. 16	11:53	12:07	12:19	12:35	12:43	12:53	13:06	13:17	13:23	13:30	13:36	13:45
Nov. 1	11:53	12:13	12:36	13:01	13:15	13:31	13:49	14:14	14:24	14:35	14:48	15:03
Nov. 16	11:53	12:21	12:50	13:22	13:42	14:03	14:29	15:00	15:14	15:30	15:49	16:09
Dec. 1	11:53	12:26	13:00	13:39	14:03	14:27	14:58	15:36	16:07	16:14	16:36	17:02
Dec. 16	11:53	12:27	13:05	13:56	14:12	14:40	15:12	15:54	16:13	16:36	17:01	17:31

Garden Size: Lighting & Yield

Size	Area	Watts	Lamp Choices	Yield (grams)
1 sq ft (0.09 sq m)	1' x 1' (0.3 x 0.3 m)	40–80w	CFLs with bowl reflectors/circular or u-tube fluorescent bulbs	10–80g
4 sq ft (0.36 sq m)	2' x 2' (0.6 x 0.6 m)	200–240w	HID (MH or HPS) T5 Fluorescents	50–250g
8 sq ft (0.75 sq m)	4' x 2' (1.25 x 0.6 m)	350–480w	T5 Fluorescents, smaller HIDs, or large HIDs on a track light shuttle	90–480g
9 sq ft (0.8 sq m)	3' x 3' (0.9 x 0.9 m)	400–600w	HPS or MH	100–600g
16 sq ft (1.55 sq m)	4' x 4' (1.25 x 1.25 m)	600–1000w	HPS or MH	300–1000g
25 sq ft (2.3 sq m)	5' x 5' (1.5 x 1.5 m)	2 x 750w (1500w)	HPS or MH	400–750g
32 sq ft (3 sq m)	4' x 8' (1.25 x 2.45 m)	3 x 600w 2 x 750w 2 x 1000w (1500–2000w)	HPS or MH	700–2000g

Note: CFL is an abbreviation for compact fluorescent lights. HID stands for High Intensity Discharge lights. The two types most commonly used in indoor gardens are MH (Metal Halide) and HPS (High Pressure Sodium).

2008 Daily UV Index

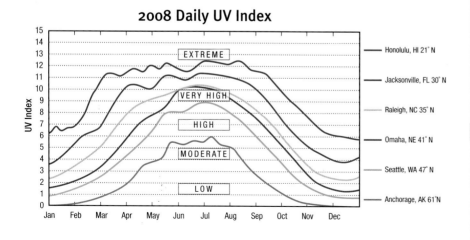

Metric Conversion

Mass

1 gram (g) =	0.035 ounces (1/28 ounce)
1 ounce (oz) =	28.35 grams
1 pound (lb) =	16 ounces
1 kilogram (kg) =	2.2 pounds
1 pound (lb) =	0.45 kilograms

Length

1 foot (ft) =	30.5 centimeters (1/3 meter)
1 meter (m) =	3.28 feet
1 meter (m) =	100 centimeters
1 inch (in) =	2.54 centimeters

Area

1 square meter (sq m) =	10.76 square feet
1 square foot (sq ft) =	0.09 square meters

Yield

1 ounce per square foot =	305 g per square meter
100 grams per square meter =	0.33 ounces per square foot

Temperature

15°C =	59°F
20°C =	68°F
25°C =	72°F
28°C =	82°F
30°C =	86°F
32°C =	89.5°F
35°C =	95°F

To Calculate:
Celsius = (F-32) x 5/9
Fahrenheit = C x 9/5 +32

Concentration
1ppm = 1 mg/L = 0.0001%

Volumes

1 teaspoon (tsp) =	5 milliliters (ml)
1 tablespoon (tbsp) =	15 milliliters (ml)
1 ounce (oz) =	30 milliliters (ml)
1 cup (c) = 8 flow ounces =	236 milliliters (ml)
1 pint (p) = 2 cups =	473 milliliters (ml)
1 quart (qt) = 2 pints =	946 milliliters (ml)
1 gallon (g) = 4 quarts =	3785 milliliters (ml) 3.785 liters (l)

Varieties by Classification

Varieties by Indica, Sativa and Ruderalis

 Indica Strains (90% to 100%)

Anesthesia
Barney's Farm Blue Cheese
Cataract Kush
Crippled Pit
Dark Star
Dready Kush
G-Bomb
Himalaya Gold
Iranian Autoflower
Kandahar
Mr. Nice
Soma-licious
Southern Nights
The OG #18
Tora Bora
Vanilla Kush

 Indica Dominant Strains (60% to 90%)

AMS
Bubble Cheese
CH9 G Bolt
Cheesus
Crystalberry
Funxta'z Purple Cali Kush
Headband

Herijuana
K-Train
Morning Star
Pit Bull
Querkle
Smoothie
Swiss Cheese
The Kali
Whitaker Blues

 Indica/Sativa Strains (50% each)

Cocoa Kush
Critical #47
Jack Flash #5
Kushadelic
L.A.P.D.
Tahoe Gold
The Ultimate
Vanilluna

 Sativa Dominant (60 to 90%)

Alaskan Ice
Apollo 13BX
Black Berry
Buddha Haze
Carnival
CH9 Flower
CH9 Jack 33
Chiesel

Sativa Dominant (60 to 90%) (con't)

Dancehall
DelaHaze
Diabolic Funxta
Green House Thai
Jamaican Pearl
Jock Horror
Lemon Skunk
Mandala #1
Mekong High
Morning Glory
Northern Light x Apollo G13
NYPD (New York Power Diesel)
Oregon Pinot Noir
Qleaner
Raspberry Cough
Skunk Haze
Sleestack
Somantra
Titan's Haze
Tropi-canna
Urban Poison
Veryberry (remix)
Vortex

 Sativa Strains (90 to 100%)

Dr. Grinspoon
Dutch Haze
Jack F6
Killing Fields

 Sativa/Indica Hybrids (% unknown)

Barney's Farm G-13 Haze

LSD
Purple Voodoo
Super Lemon Haze

 Ruderalis and Ruderalis Hybrids

Angelmatic (S/I/R)
Automaria (I/R)
Easy Rider (I/S/R)
Iranian Autoflower (I/R)
PolarLight (S/R)
SnowStorm (I/R)
Taiga (S/I/R)
Tundra (I/R)

 Autoflower

Angelmatic
Automaria
Easy Rider
Iranian Autoflower
PolarLight
SnowStorm
Taiga
Tundra

Varieties by Environment

Indoor Strains

Anesthesia
Black Berry
Bubble Cheese
Buddha Haze
Dark Star
Dutch Haze

Green House Thai
Herijuana
Jack F6
Jock Horror
Killing Fields
NYPD (New York Power Diesel)
Raspberry Cough
Skunk Haze
Urban Poison

 Outdoor Strains

Critical #47
Easy Rider
Iranian Autoflower

 Indoor/Outdoor Strains

Alaskan Ice
AMS
Angelmatic
Apollo 13BX
Automaria
Barney's Farm Blue Cheese
Barney's Farm G-13 Haze
Carnival
Cataract Kush
CH9 Flower
CH9 G Bolt
CH9 Jack 33
Cheesus
Chiesel
Cocoa Kush
Crippled Pit
Crystalberry

Dancehall
DelaHaze
Diabolic Funxta
Dr. Grinspoon
Dready Kush
Funxta'z Purple Cali Kush
G-Bomb
Headband
Himalaya Gold
Jack Flash #5
Jamaican Pearl
K-Train
Kandahar
L.A.P.D.
Lemon Skunk
LSD
Mandala #1
Mekong High
Morning Glory
Morning Star
Mr. Nice
Northern Light x Apollo G13
Oregon Pinot Noir
Pit Bull
PolarLight
Purple Voodoo
Qleaner
Querkle
Sleestack
Smoothie
SnowStorm
Soma-licious
Somantra

Indoor/Outdoor Strains (con't.)

Southern Nights
Super Lemon Haze
Swiss Cheese
Tahoe Gold
Taiga
The OG #18
Titan's Haze
Tundra
The Kali
The Ultimate
Tora Bora
Tropi-canna
Vanilla Kush
Vanilluna
Veryberry (remix)
Vortex
Whitaker Blues

Greenhouse Recommended Varieties
Dutch Haze
L.A.P.D.
Mekong High
The Ultimate

 ## Sea of Green Recommended Varieties
Anesthesia
Angelmatic
Apollo 13BX
Automaria
Barney's Farm G-13 Haze
Black Berry

Bubble Cheese
Carnival
Cataract Kush
CH9 Flower
CH9 G Bolt
Cheesus
Chiesel
Cocoa Kush
Critical #47
Crystalberry
Dancehall
Dready Kush
Easy Rider
G-Bomb
Headband
Herijuana
Iranian Autoflower
Jack F6
Jack Flash #5
Jamaican Pearl
Jock Horror
K-Train
Killing Fields
Kushadelic
L.A.P.D.
LSD
Mandala #1
Mr. Nice
Northern Light x Apollo G13
NYPD (New York Power Diesel)
PolarLight
Purple Voodoo
Querkle
Raspberry Cough

Sleestack
Smoothie
Southern Nights
Swiss Cheese
Tahoe Gold
The Kali
The OG #18
Titan's Haze
Tropi-canna
Urban Poison
Vanilluna
Whitaker Blues

 ## Screen of Green Recommended Varieties

Alaskan Ice
AMS
Anesthesia
Apollo 13BX
Barney's Farm Blue Cheese
Barney's Farm G-13 Haze
Black Berry
Bubble Cheese
Buddha Haze
Carnival
CH9 Flower
CH9 G Bolt
CH9 Jack 33
Cheesus
Chiesel
Cocoa Kush
DelaHaze
Diabolic Funxta
Funxta'z Purple Cali Kush

G-Bomb
Green House Thai
Headband
Herijuana
Himalaya Gold
Jack F6
Jack Flash #5
Jamaican Pearl
K-Train
Kandahar
Killing Fields
L.A.P.D.
Lemon Skunk
LSD
Mandala #1
Mekong High
Morning Glory
Morning Star
Northern Light x Apollo G13
NYPD (New York Power Diesel)
Oregon Pinot Noir
Pit Bull
Purple Voodoo
Qleaner
Querkle
Skunk Haze
Smoothie
Soma-licious
Somantra
Super Lemon Haze
Swiss Cheese
Tahoe Gold
Tundra
The Kali

Screen of Green Recommended Varieties (con't)

The OG #18
The Ultimate
Tropi-canna
Vanilla Kush
Veryberry (remix)
Vortex
Urban Poison
Vanilluna
Whitaker Blues

Feminized

Alaskan Ice
AMS
Angelmatic
Barney's Farm Blue Cheese
Barney's Farm G-13 Haze
Black Berry
Bubble Cheese
Buddha Haze
Carnival
Cataract Kush
CH9 Flower
CH9 G Bolt
CH9 Jack 33
Cheesus
Chiesel
Critical #47
Dancehall
DelaHaze
Dr. Grinspoon
Dutch Haze
Easy Rider

G-Bomb
Green House Thai
Headband
Himalaya Gold
Iranian Autoflower
Jack Flash #5
Jock Horror
K-Train
Kandahar
Kushadelic
Lemon Skunk
LSD
Mekong High
Morning Glory
Northern Light x Apollo G13
NYPD (New York Power Diesel)
PolarLight
Raspberry Cough
Skunk Haze
Sleestack
SnowStorm
Somantra
Southern Nights
Super Lemon Haze
Swiss Cheese
Taiga
The Kali
The OG #18
The Ultimate
Tora Bora
Tropi-canna
Tundra
Urban Poison
Vanilla Kush

Thanks to all of the businesses, organizations and individuals that supported this project.

The Big Book of **BUDS**

volume 4

Marijuana Varieties from the World's Great Seed Breeders

Hash Marihuana & Hemp Museum

A M S T E R D A M

A PERMANENT EXHIBITION ABOUT THE HISTORY
AND USE OF CANNABIS AROUND THE WORLD.

Hash Marihuana & Hemp Museum

Oudezijds Achterburgwal 148 Amsterdam

Open every day from 10.00 AM till 23.00 PM

www.hashmuseum.com

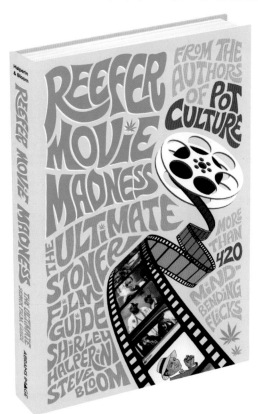

HASHBAR.TV

Tommy Chong from Cheech and Chong and Sean Kush

T.N.A. World Champion Rob Van Dam, B Real from Cypress Hill and Sean Kush

Five time W.C.W. World Champion Booker T and Sean Kush

Pinapple Kush girl and Sean Kush at the T.H.C. expose 2010.

An assortment of some of the best medical marijuana in the world!

The ultimate Cheech and Chong porn star hash joint. 2 ounces of porn star kush and 5 grams of hash. 2 hours to roll and 3 hours to smoke.

Oxygen ear wax hash. Very potent! Watch it bubble.

Sean Kush: as featured in the June 6, 2010 L.A Times.

Edible girl from the T.H.C. expose 2010.

Go to www.hashbar.tv every week for new episodes

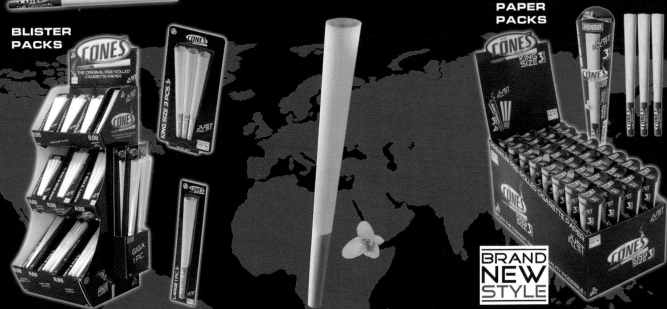
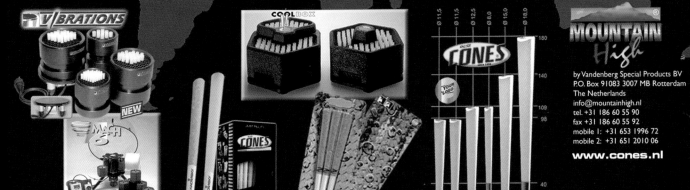

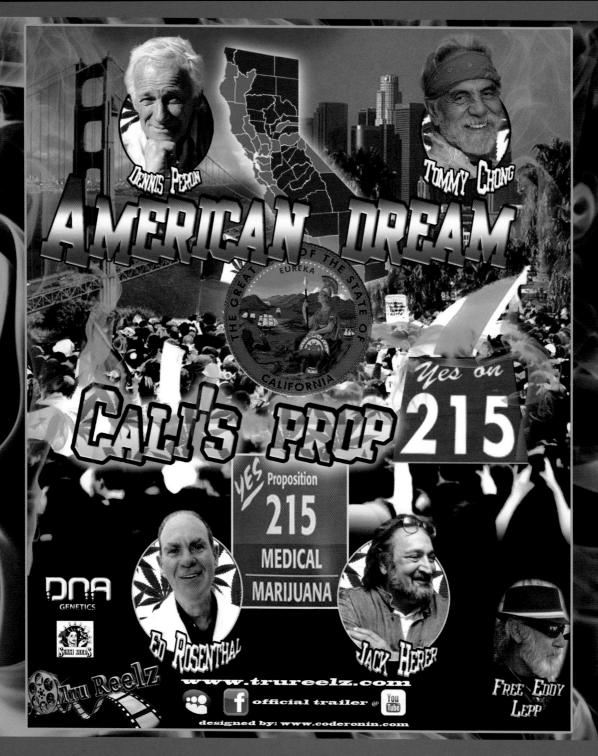

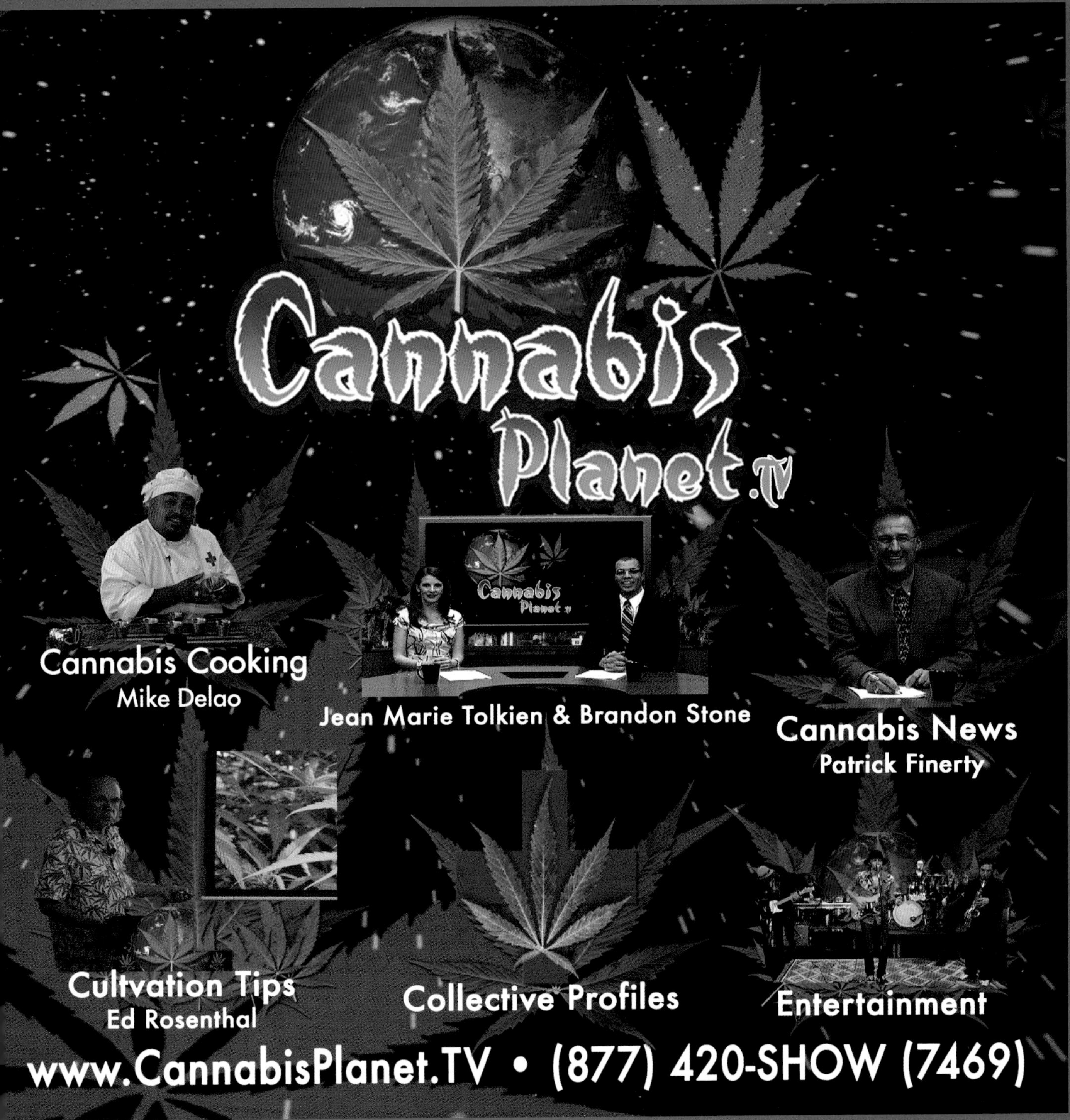

Cannabis Planet.TV

Cannabis Cooking
Mike Delao

Jean Marie Tolkien & Brandon Stone

Cannabis News
Patrick Finerty

Cultvation Tips
Ed Rosenthal

Collective Profiles

Entertainment

www.CannabisPlanet.TV • (877) 420-SHOW (7469)

WWW.QUICKTRADING.COM
ONLINE HOME OF ASK ED™
Marijuana Questions?
Come Online and Ask Ed
BOOKS AND GUIDES · GROW TIPS · BUD SHOTS

BARNEY's
UpTown
AMSTERDAM

OPEN FOR BREAKFAST, LUNCH & HEDONISTIC INDULGENCE

EVERY DAY FROM 7AM TILL VERY LATE

HAARLEMMERSTRAAT 105 AMSTERDAM

WWW.BARNEYS.BIZ

Strain Type

Sativa

Indica

Indica/Sativa

Sativa/Indica

Sativa/Ruderalis

Indica/Ruderalis

Sativa/Indica/Ruderalis

Feminized

Autoflowering

Growing Info

Flowering Time
Tiempo de floración
Blütezeit
Durée de floraison
Stagione della fioritura
Bloetijd

Parentage
Genética
Mutterpflanze
Descendance
Genitori
Stamboom

Yield
Rendimiento
Ertag
Rendement
Raccolta
Opbrengst

Indoor
Interior
Drinnen
D'Intérieur
Dentro
Binnen

Outdoor
Exterior
Draussen
d'Extérieur
Fuori
Buiten

Indoor/Outdoor
Interior/Exterior
Drinnen/Draussen
d'Intérieur/d'Extérieur
Dentro/Fuori
Binnen/Buiten

SOG
Sea of Green

Screen of Green

Sensory Experience

Buzz
Efecto
die Art des Turns
Effets
Effetti
High Effekt

Taste/Smell
Sabor/Aroma
Geschmack/Geruch
Saveur/Arôme
Sapore/Odore
Smaak/Geua

Breeder Location

Canada

Netherlands

Spain

United Kingdom

U.S.A.

Strain Diary

Strain name: ....

Date: ....

Smell: ....

Taste: ....

Buzz: ....

Notes: ....

Strain name: ....

Date: ....

Smell: ....

Taste: ....

Buzz: ....

Notes: ....

Strain name: ....

Date: ....

Smell: ....

Taste: ....

Buzz: ....

Notes: ....

Strain name: ....

Date: ....

Smell: ....

Taste: ....

Buzz: ....

Notes: ....

Strain name: ....

Date: ....

Smell: ....

Taste: ....

Buzz: ....

Notes: ....

Strain name: ....

Date: ....

Smell: ....

Taste: ....

Buzz: ....

Notes: ....

Strain name: ....

Date: ....

Smell: ....

Taste: ....

Buzz: ....

Notes: ....

Strain name: ....

Date: ....

Smell: ....

Taste: ....

Buzz: ....

Notes: ....

Strain name: ....

Date: ....

Smell: ....

Taste: ....

Buzz: ....

Notes: ....

Strain name: ....

Date: ....

Smell: ....

Taste: ....

Buzz: ....

Notes: ....

Strain name: ....

Date: ....

Smell: ....

Taste: ....

Buzz: ....

Notes: ....

Strain name: ....

Date: ....

Smell: ....

Taste: ....

Buzz: ....

Notes: ....